GW00535575

C31904

Collateral Warranties Explained

Collateral Warranties Explained

Frances A. Paterson

© 1991 Frances A. Paterson

Published by RIBA Publications Ltd
Finsbury Mission, Moreland Street, London EC1V 8BB

RIBA Publications is the publishing subsidiary of
the Royal Institute of British Architects

ISBN 0 947877 57 6

All rights reserved. No part of this publication may be reproduced, stored in a
retrieval system, or transmitted, in any form or by any means, electronic,
mechanical, photocopying, recording or otherwise, without the prior permission of
the copyright owner.

Editor: Alaine Hamilton
Index compiled by Richard Raper, Indexing Specialists
Book design and computer page make-up: Penny Mills
Printed and bound by Billing & Sons Ltd, Worcester

Whilst every effort has been made to check the accuracy of the
information given in this book, readers should always make their
own checks. Neither the author nor the publisher accepts any
responsibility for mis-statements made in it or misunderstandings
arising from it.

The various personae in this book are referred to as 'he', purely as
a matter of stylistic simplicity.

Contents

Preface

Many architects are being asked to sign collateral warranties, and they may do so without fully understanding their implications. This book explains, in plain English, what collateral warranties are and gives architects some appreciation of the liabilities they are undertaking.

Any architect who is asked to sign a collateral warranty would be well advised to seek legal advice. This book cannot be a substitute for that. The practice relating to warranties (and to some extent the law as well) is constantly changing and it is important for an architect to be aware of the up-to-date position. Examples of typical clauses have been given, wherever possible, but they are examples not precedents.

The law discussed is that applicable to England and Wales; the law in Scotland is different in certain respects.

This book is addressed to architects but most of what is said is equally relevant to other members of the design team, even though the roles they perform and the services they undertake are different.

The writing of this book has been greatly assisted by Gillian Birkby, a solicitor and partner in the construction department of Rowe & Maw. She has provided legal material, corrected and edited the text and given invaluable support and encouragement throughout.

Frances A. Paterson
April 1991

Glossary and definitions

Readers may not be familiar with some of the legal terminology used. Generally, when a term is first employed, an explanation is included in the text. Some non-legal words are used in a particular sense in the book, and a definition is therefore included here.

Assignee
A party to whom something is assigned.

Assignor
A party who assigns something.

Case law
Judgments given by the Courts in particular cases (see the examples in the case notes, section 9).

Cause of action
All the facts needed by a plaintiff to prove that a defendant owes him a duty and that he has committed a breach of that duty; thus a cause of action accrues when those facts have occurred.

Collateral warranty
A form of contract collateral to (ie alongside) another contract (see paragraph 1.08).

Common law
Used in this book to refer to case law (see above) as opposed to statute law, although it can have a wider meaning.

Consideration
A benefit given by one party to another. It is a legal requirement for the formation of a valid contract, other than a deed (see paragraph 1.18).

Developer
In this book, a party undertaking a development or project.

Financier
In this book, a party lending finance for the construction of a development but not acquiring a freehold or leasehold interest (see paragraph 2.12).

Fund
In this book, a party lending finance for the construction of a development and also acquiring the freehold, ie a forward funding purchaser (see paragraph 2.12).

Limitation period

The time limit within which legal proceedings must be commenced. It often begins on the date of the accrual of the cause of action (see above), for example, the date of the breach of contract.

Negligence

An abbreviation of the 'tort of negligence' (see below). Not to be confused with the fact that someone can be negligent in contract as well as tort if they are in breach of a contractual obligation not to be negligent.

Promisor

A person who makes a promise.

Promisee

A person to whom a promise is made.

Purchaser

In this book, a party acquiring a development (generally the freehold, but it could be a long leasehold) by purchase.

Reliance duty

A duty of care in tort not to act negligently, which arises when a party possessing special skill or knowledge gives information or advice which he should know will be relied upon by another (see *Hedley Byrne v Heller*, case notes paragraph 9.14).

Tenant

In this book, a party taking a lease of a development.

Tort

A civil wrong, independent of contract. There are a number of torts, including negligence, nuisance and defamation, which the Courts recognise as entitling the wronged party to bring a legal action against the wrongdoer. The tort of negligence is often referred to simply as 'tort' or 'negligence'.

Warrantee

A party obtaining the benefit of a warranty (for example, a financier, purchaser or tenant).

Warrantor

A party giving a warranty (for example, an architect).

Warranty

Often used to mean collateral warranty (see above), which is how the term is used in this book. It also refers to a type of clause in a contract.

1 Introduction

The need for warranties

1.01 In July 1990 the House of Lords, in giving judgment in a construction case, held that a decision reached by the House some thirteen years earlier and applied in numerous subsequent cases, had been wrongly decided. Nothing more vividly demonstrates the changes that have occurred in recent years in the law of the tort of negligence.

1.02 This recent case, and others, have curtailed remedies in tort. As a result numerous parties (other than the immediate client) who acquire an interest in a development are seeking to obtain contracts – called collateral warranties – from architects and other members of the design and construction team.

1.03 The problem, in the most general terms, is this: who should carry the risk (in other words, bear the cost) of latent defects, that is defects appearing in a development after completion? To what extent should those who suffer loss as a result of those defects, other than the original developer, be able to recover damages from the design and construction team? Warranties are all about the allocation of this risk.

1.04 Architects can be liable for their mistakes in contract, in tort or under statute. With regard to contract, the practice has changed dramatically over the last five years or so. It used to be the case that virtually all architectural commissions were undertaken on terms which originated from the architect, often by an exchange of letters, perhaps incorporating the *Architect's Appointment* published by the RIBA. Now, it is common for architects to be sent non-standard terms of considerable length and complexity. In addition, architects are being asked to sign further, collateral, contracts or warranties in favour of certain third parties.

1.05 With regard to the tort of negligence (often referred to simply as 'tort' or 'negligence'), the change is in the law itself (see case notes, section 9). Much of English law derives from cases which have come before the courts and set a precedent, and this is particularly true of tort. Recent decisions have severely restricted – or appear to have severely restricted – liabilities in tort. The law has changed, but at the same time it is uncertain exactly what rights anyone has in tort. It is for this reason that people do not wish to rely on tortious remedies, and seek contractual ones.

1.06   With regard to statute, under the Defective Premises Act 1972, architects have certain statutory obligations in relation to services they provide in relation to dwellings, but the Act does not apply to any other type of building (see paragraph 2.24). There are at present no plans for further legislation.

1.07   As will be explained, a warranty is a contract granting rights that until comparatively recently existed in tort. In the absence of widely accepted standard forms, parties usually negotiate the terms of warranties on a project by project basis. Thus, the parties themselves undertake the risk allocation exercise that was the function of the common law. The result can be a very different allocation of risk, often to the disadvantage of the architect. As will be seen, there are also a number of pitfalls for the unwary in replacing tortious remedies by contractual ones.

What a collateral warranty is

1.08   'Collateral warranty', as the term is used in the construction industry, is a name for a form of contract which is collateral to (ie alongside) another contract. The terminology used can be confusing. These contracts have come to be generally known as collateral warranties, or warranties, but they may be given a variety of titles (for example, duty of care deeds, deeds of responsibility, memoranda of agreement, or something of that kind). Since they are often known simply as 'warranties' that is how they will be described in this book. In the case of an architect, a warranty is collateral to his terms of engagement and in the case of a contractor, it is collateral to the building contract. (The term 'warranty', as used by lawyers, also has another technical meaning, referring to a category of clauses in a contract, but this is not the way in which the term is used in this book.)

1.09   A warranty creates a contractual relationship where otherwise none would usually exist. For example, if an architect is engaged by a developer who then sells the newly constructed building, and the architect gives a warranty to the purchaser, a contract between the architect and the purchaser is created. The reason why the purchaser seeks this contract, or warranty, from the architect is that, without it, he is not certain that he would have a remedy against the architect in the event that he suffers loss as a result of the architect's negligence. Until recently, he would have relied on having a remedy in the tort of negligence, but case law has now considerably reduced liabilities in tort (see case notes, section 9).

1.10   Although warranties between the professional team and those who finance, buy or lease developments are comparatively new, warranties in the context of construction are not. For example, architects' warranties have a similar effect as a warranty between an employer and a nominated or domestic sub-contractor, such as that used with the JCT Standard Form of Building Contract, 1980 Edition (JCT 80). The employer has a contract with the main contractor, who in turn has a contract with the sub-contractor. The warranty creates a direct contractual link between the employer and the sub-contractor, in the same way that an architect–purchaser warranty creates a direct contractual link.

1.11   As explained above, warranties may be given a variety of titles. They may also be in a number of different formats. Warranties are generally set out as agreements or deeds or, occasionally, as letters. However, whatever their appearance, the legal effect will depend upon whether the document is a simple contract (as lawyers call it), a deed or some other document.

1.12   On page 34 there is an example of a warranty set out as a simple contract (often called an agreement). A simple contract requires 'consideration' (see paragraphs 1.18 and 5.06) but no formalities regarding execution are necessary.

1.13   For a warranty to be a deed, the formalities regarding execution must be complied with (see paragraph 1.21) but on the other hand there is no need for consideration. It will be seen, from the example shown on page 35, that a deed is now generally only signed (not signed and sealed as was the case until recently, see paragraph 1.21) but the difference from a simple contract lies in the words above the signatures *In witness whereof the parties hereto have executed this document as a deed* and the fact that the signatures have to be witnessed etc. The essential characteristic of a deed, therefore, is the attestation clause (which appears at the end). This means that a warranty can look like a letter but have the legal effect of a deed if it is appropriately executed.

1.14   The two examples on pages 34 and 35 illustrate the form and language that is generally, but not invariably, used for simple contracts (agreements) and deeds respectively.

Simple contracts

1.15   There are three requirements for the formation of a valid contract and, therefore, a warranty: offer and acceptance, consideration (unless it is a deed), and the intention to create legal relations.

1.16   The first requirement is that there should be an offer, on terms which are certain, which is accepted. In the case of a warranty the offer and acceptance will usually be evidenced by both the person giving the warranty (for example, an architect) and the beneficiary being parties to and signing the warranty and this is the most straightforward course.

1.17   A warranty could be in the form of a letter from the warrantor (the architect) to the warrantee (the purchaser, for example). It is more usual for it to be in the form of an agreement (or deed, see paragraph 1.20) in which case both the architect and purchaser (and sometimes the client as well, see paragraph 5.03) will be parties. The architect will be asked to sign the warranty and the simplest and safest course is for the other party (or parties) to sign it as well. If the warrantee has any obligations (eg to pay copying charges) then he should certainly be asked to sign the warranty.

1.18   The second requirement for a valid contract, the need for consideration, means that – in the simplest terms – a purely gratuitous promise is not enforceable as a contract. The most obvious form of consideration is the payment of a sum of money in exchange for a promise to supply or do something, but it can take other forms. If the consideration is the payment of a sum of money but it is not paid, the contract is not rendered invalid, but the party undertaking to pay the consideration is in breach of contract and the party who is to receive it can demand that it be paid. The consideration need not be expressed in the document itself, but it is preferable that it is. (See paragraph 5.06 for an example of a consideration clause). If the consideration is the payment of money, a nominal sum will suffice. Recent case law suggests that the courts might take a more liberal view than they did of what constitutes 'sufficient' consideration.

1.19   The third requirement, an intention to create legal relations, speaks for itself. It can be presumed, in the case of a warranty signed by both parties, or offered by one and accepted by the other. However, a 'letter of comfort' (see paragraph 1.27) might not constitute a valid contract both because it lacks consideration and because it does not evidence an intention to create legal relations.

Deeds

1.20   A deed is a formal contract and some types of transaction, for example in relation to the disposal of land, have to be by deed rather than simple contract. The distinguishing features of a deed, in this context, are firstly that the limitation period (that is, in effect, the time limit for pursuing a claim) is twelve years from the date of the breach of contract, as opposed to six years in the case of a simple contract, and secondly that it is enforceable without consideration.

1.21   The law relating to the execution of deeds has been changed by section 1 of the Law of Property (Miscellaneous Provisions) Act 1989 (in the case of individuals) and by section 130 of the Companies Act 1989 (in the case of companies). Reference should now be made to deeds rather than contracts under seal (which is how they used to be described) as the need for a seal has been abolished for this purpose.

1.22   In the case of an individual, for a document to be valid as a deed after 31 July 1990 (the date on which the section came into force) it must comply with that section. It must be clear on its face that it is intended to be a deed: in the words of section 1(2)(a) 'whether by describing itself as a deed or expressing itself to be executed or signed as a deed or otherwise'. It must also be validly executed as a deed, that is, it must be signed in the presence of a witness who attests the signature and it must be delivered as a deed by the signatory or an authorised person on his behalf.

1.23   Preferably the document itself should be described as a deed at the beginning and, where necessary, in the body of the document (as, for example, *as expressly provided in this Deed*). An example of an attestation clause for an individual is set out in the example on page 35.

1.24   The new rules relating to the execution of deeds by companies are similar and came into force on the same day. A company is no longer required to have a company seal for this purpose, although it may have one. A deed may therefore be validly executed by a company by the affixing of its company seal (if it has one) and (subject to anything to the contrary contained in its articles of association) by being signed by a director and the secretary or by two directors, but it must also be expressed to be executed as a deed and be delivered. (Rules relating to delivery are set out in section 130 of the Companies Act 1989). An example of an attestation clause for a company which does not have or does not wish to use its company seal is also set out in the example on page 35. If the company does use its seal, the clause would have to be appropriately adapted.

Other documents

1.25   If a document (not being a deed) sets out an obligation but there is no consideration mentioned, it may not be enforceable as a contract. The question then arises whether it is legally enforceable at all. Documents described as duty of care letters or letters of comfort might come into this category.

1.26   First, a court might look for some consideration even if it is not expressed in the document itself. Alternatively, it is possible that such a document might form the basis of a 'reliance duty', akin to that which could have been owed by the bank which gave a reference in the leading case of *Hedley Byrne v Heller* (see case notes, 9.14). An example of this would be an architect being asked to write a letter to a tenant to whom a development had been pre-let, confirming that the tenant was relying on the architect's skill and judgment. Such a letter could possibly result in the architect undertaking liabilities which he had not anticipated. Indeed, the liabilities could be more onerous than those undertaken in some warranties.

1.27   A letter of comfort might be literally no more than that, but it would be unwise for an architect to assume that a warranty in such a form had no legal effect, simply because those drafting it forgot to include a consideration clause. (For an example of a letter of comfort that had to be considered by the Court of Appeal before its effect could be ascertained see *Kleinwort Benson Ltd v Malaysian Mining Corporation.*)

2 Who might be asked to give a warranty and who might seek one?

Who might be asked to give a warranty?

2.01 Warranties may be sought from anyone – consultants or contractors – who might cause substantial loss by their negligence or breach of contract.

2.02 On the one hand there is the design team, and this may include architect, structural engineer, mechanical and electrical engineer, quantity surveyor, project manager and others with a less central role. All might be asked to give warranties.

2.03 On the other hand there is the contracting team. For the beneficiary to be fully protected, warranties would be needed from all those with primary responsibility for the construction or design. Who this includes will vary according to the form of the building contract and the method of building procurement.

2.04 First, in the case of the traditional method of building procurement, for example using JCT 80, the main contractor is fully responsible for the standard of workmanship and quality of materials for all the works on site, including those of his sub-contractors and suppliers. However, he is not usually responsible for any design undertaken by them, unless the Contractor's Designed Portion Supplement is used. If there is a nominated sub-contractor who undertakes design, it is good practice for an employer–sub-contractor warranty to be signed, because the main contractor is not liable for the design work of nominated sub-contractors (even when the Contractor's Designed Portion Supplement has been used) and an employer will have little remedy in respect of a nominated sub-contractor's negligent design without such a warranty. In the same way, if a party who purchases a completed development wants to have rights of recovery against a nominated sub-contractor in relation to design, he will need to obtain a warranty from the nominated sub-contractor since a warranty from the main contractor will not suffice. Further, if a domestic sub-contractor or supplier is carrying out design, a purchaser may possibly require a warranty from him.

2.05   Secondly, in the case of management contracting, for example using the JCT Management Contract, 1987 Edition (MC 87), by the terms of the contract the management contractor is liable for all the work carried out by works contractors – including design, where appropriate. However, the management contract also contains a proviso that the management contractor is not liable to the employer for a defaulting works contractor except to the extent that he can and has recovered damages in respect of that liability from the works contractor. In other words, the management contractor is only liable to pay damages to the employer if he has recovered those damages from the defaulting works contractor. Thus when a management contractor gives a warranty, the exact wording will be crucial in determining the extent of his liability. The warrantee will want to ensure that the management contractor cannot avoid liability under the warranty simply because he is unable to recover from a defaulting works contractor. Under this form of contract, therefore, a prudent financier, purchaser or tenant may seek warranties from all the works contractors, if the terms of the management contractor's warranty restrict his liability to that which he has for works contractors under the management contract. Obtaining warranties from all the works contractors could be a time-consuming process.

2.06   Thirdly, in the case of construction management there is a problem in this context. In this form of contracting (in the sense in which the term is generally used) the employer engages a construction manager. The employer also engages the contractors who are to undertake the on-site works (generally known as trade contractors) directly. They are not employed by the construction manager. Thus, the construction manager is merely the agent of the developer and has no contractual liability for the work of the trade contractors, and if a purchaser acquiring the development wants contractual rights against those responsible for the on-site works, he needs to obtain warranties from every trade contractor. On a large project, there could be a considerable number of these.

2.07   Fourthly, in the case of design and build the main contractor will have responsibility for all the design (to the extent set out in the contract) and the construction. Therefore, by obtaining a warranty from the contractor a purchaser has full protection, so long as the contractor is worth suing. The contractor may use in-house design expertise or employ independent firms of consultants as design sub-contractors, in which case the consultants, including the architect, may be asked to give the employer a warranty.

2.08   There are two schools of thought about the need for a warranty between the architect and the employer. The first is that it is not necessary, and could be disadvantageous. One reason for adopting design and build is that there is only one party liable whatever type of problem arises and this advantage is in part lost if a warranty is obtained. With two parties liable (one under the design and build contract and the other under a warranty) they will doubtless both be brought into any proceedings, which can therefore become more protracted and expensive. The second school of thought is that it is a wise precaution for the employer to obtain a warranty from the architect, since he then has some remedy if the contractor proves to be insolvent and not worth suing.

2.09   Similar arguments apply if an architect is asked to give a warranty to anyone else, eg a purchaser, tenant or financier. If the design and build contractor gives them warranties, they will encompass the design undertaken by the architect. The purchaser or tenant does not need the warranty in the sense that he has a remedy against the design and build contractor in respect of negligent design. However, the additional protection of a warranty from the architect may be requested as a precaution against the contractor's insolvency.

Who might seek a warranty?

2.10   Warranties are sought by those who acquire an interest in a development and who would not, in the absence of a warranty, have a contract with those responsible for the design and construction. Architects are asked to give warranties by clients undertaking certain kinds of developments for which they obtain finance, or which they might wish to sell or lease at some time.

2.11   Those requiring warranties can be split into the following categories: financiers; non-occupiers (including funding purchasers); occupiers (purchasers or tenants); others (for example land owners who have entered into development agreements and employers of design and build contractors); and lastly those who own or occupy dwellings.

FINANCIERS

2.12   The term 'financier' is used here to mean a party lending finance
for a development but not acquiring a freehold or leasehold
interest. A financier will probably therefore have a legal charge
over the land and the development on it in the same way that a
mortgagee does, although other security might be offered. A
financier is differentiated from a mortgagee, in that the former
lends finance for the purpose of undertaking and completing a
development, whereas a mortgagee lends money on the security of
a finished development. To avoid confusion the term 'fund' is used
in this book to mean a party lending finance for the project and
also acquiring the ownership, ie a purchaser who is making
forward funding available. In practice, the terms 'financier' and
'fund' are used in either sense.

2.13   Finance arrangements vary enormously: the loan might be
repayable once the project is sold, the intention being that it
should not be retained by the developer beyond practical
completion, or the loan repayment period might be spread over
many years. In any event, however, a financier will be concerned
that all goes well with the construction, so that his security
achieves its expected value and he can be repaid his loan. One of
his principal requirements will be the right to step in and take over
the appointment of consultants and contractor in order to
complete the development in the event of a default by the
employer under the funding agreement (see paragraph 5.81).

2.14   A standard form of warranty to be given by consultants only (not
contractors) to financiers (not funds, see paragraph 2.12), has been
agreed between the British Property Federation, the Royal
Institute of British Architects, the Association of Consulting
Engineers and the Royal Institution of Chartered Surveyors, and
was published in May 1990. It is referred to in this book as the
'BPF financier's warranty'.

NON-OCCUPIERS

2.15   The term 'non-occupier' is used here to mean a party with a
freehold or leasehold interest in a development who is not an
occupier and does not have the primary obligation to put right
latent defects. Typically this is an investment purchaser who has
(or will) let the development on full repairing and insuring leases.

2.16   A non-occupying purchaser could be a fund, in the sense that it
        may have forward-funded the development with an agreement that
        it will acquire the ownership upon satisfactory completion (see
        paragraph 2.12). A fund will probably require step-in rights in the
        same way as a financier generally does. The difference between a
        financier and a fund is important in relation to the question of
        damages recoverable (see paragraph 5.34).

        OCCUPIERS

2.17   The term 'occupier' is used to mean a party who has a freehold or
        leasehold interest in the property, is occupying it for his own use,
        and has the responsibility to remedy latent defects. He will either be,
        first, an owner occupier who has acquired the development from the
        developer (ie a purchaser). Secondly, he may be a tenant who has
        responsibility for remedying latent defects because his lease includes
        a full repairing and insuring covenant (known as a full repairing
        and insuring lease), or an obligation to reimburse the landlord for
        the cost of making good latent defects (a full recovery lease).
        Tenants, whatever the size and value of their interest, are commonly
        asked to sign this type of lease, and therefore they will wish to
        protect themselves against the cost of remedying latent defects. Any
        other tenant, for instance one whose responsibility is limited to
        maintaining the property in good repair, will not need warranties.

2.18   It is usual for warranties to be offered to first purchasers and first
        tenants only. Subsequent purchasers or tenants will therefore either
        have no warranty or will take an assignment of the warranty given
        to the first purchaser or first tenant (see paragraph 5.57).

2.19   One particularly difficult question is whether there should be a
        limit on the size of the occupier's interest in a development below
        which he will not be entitled to a warranty. This is a particular
        problem in the case of tenants. Some would argue that any tenant,
        however small the unit he is leasing, is entitled to a warranty. The
        result of this could be that, on a large project, hundreds of
        warranties might have to be given. Consider the example of a
        multi-let shopping centre development undertaken on a
        construction management contract. In practical terms, this is an
        exceptionally cumbersome way of dealing with the question of
        allocation of risk.

2.20   A formula sometimes employed by those being asked to provide warranties is that they will only give them to tenants taking the whole or a substantial part of the development.

OTHERS

2.21 Warranties might be sought by, for example, the owner of land who has entered into a development agreement with the architect's client. His position would be similar to that of a fund (ie a non-occupying investment purchaser) if he is not going to occupy the development himself, or an occupier if he is.

2.22 Another example of someone who might request a warranty is a developer who has let the development to a tenant who is carrying out extensive fitting-out works: the landlord developer might seek a warranty from the architect engaged by the tenant. A further example is the employer of a design and build contractor who in turn has employed an architect. Although the contractor will have responsibility for the design, the employer might wish to take the precaution of obtaining a direct warranty from the contractor's architect (see paragraph 2.08).

2.23 Other more unusual requests for warranties are sometimes made, for example for sub-tenants, a purchaser's mortgagee, or companies in the same group as the client company.

OWNERS AND OCCUPIERS OF DWELLINGS

2.24 The Defective Premises Act 1972 imposes certain statutory obligations on those who design and build dwellings, including architects. The Act applies to dwellings only and not to any other kind of buildings.

2.25 *D & F Estates* was a case concerning a dwelling, a flat with defective ceiling and wall plaster (see case notes, 9.05). The Court of Appeal made the point that although the Act did not apply to that particular case (because the cause of action had arisen before the Act came into force) if such an issue were to arise now, the tenant would have a statutory remedy.

2.26 The duty is owed, by section 1(1) of the Act, *by a person taking on work for or in connection with the provision of a dwelling.* This would include both an architect and a contractor. It applies *whether the dwelling is provided by the erection or by the conversion or enlargement of the building*, meaning that it would cover a small back extension and the conversion of a barn into a house as well as a new mansion or a block of flats. It would also cover the residential element of a larger development. The duty is owed

(a) *if the dwelling is provided to the order of any person, to that person*; and

(b) *without prejudice to paragraph (a) above, to every person who acquires an interest (whether legal or equitable) in the dwelling.* In other words, it is owed to the client himself, as well as to subsequent owners and occupiers.

2.27　The duty is to see that the work which he takes on is done in a workmanlike or, as the case may be, professional manner with proper materials and so that as regards that work the dwelling will be fit for habitation when completed. Undertaking work in a professional manner presumably requires the usual standard of care for professional persons of reasonable skill and care (as opposed to any higher standard), although there is no reported case on the point. The requirement is only that the dwelling be fit for habitation. Doubtless, in the fullness of time, a body of case law will grow up which will amplify what this means.

2.28　The Act prohibits any attempt to exclude its operation, for example in a contract. There is, though, a provision that the Act does not apply if the dwelling is subject to a scheme approved under the Act. There is sometimes some confusion as to whether the warranty scheme operated by the National House Building Council is approved. The answer is that the schemes dated 1973, 1975 and 1977 are, but the more recent ones are not. The effect of this, therefore, is that if a dwelling is covered by an NHBC certificate issued under one of these schemes, the architect cannot be sued under the Act, because it does not apply.

2.29　The limitation period under the Act is six years from the date on which the dwelling was completed.

3 When might a warranty be called for?

3.01   When asked by his client to execute a warranty, an architect will first of all want to ascertain whether he is under a legal obligation to do so. Even if he is not, he may decide to accommodate his client's request for commercial reasons, but in that case he may have more bargaining power about the terms of the warranty.

The contractual obligation to give warranties

3.02   In deciding whether or not an architect is under a legal obligation to give a warranty, the first question is whether he has concluded a contract with his client. If he has, the second question is whether the contract includes a commitment to provide warranties. If it does, the third question is whether the commitment is to give a warranty to the proposed beneficiary, and in the form proposed. In other words, is the architect legally bound to give a warranty, to this party, in this form?

3.03   Taking these points in turn: first, whether there is a concluded contract between the architect and his client may not be an easy question to answer. If there is a formal agreement of some kind, the answer is plain enough. However, not infrequently (particularly on jobs begun in the mid 1980s, at a time of boom) there is no formally agreed document. In that case, if there is a concluded contract it will be contained in, or evidenced by, the correspondence. It is not unknown for there to be no finally concluded contract at all, even though the architect may have been working on a project for some time.

3.04   All that is needed to form the contract of appointment is an offer incorporating all the necessary terms, and an acceptance of those terms. The contract does not even have to be in writing. If, say, the architect and his client have a meeting at the beginning of the project and agree all the terms of the contract (for example, what the architect is to do and what he is to be paid), a binding contract is formed there and then. However, in practice it will be difficult to prove what the terms are unless they are put in writing, and therefore it is as well for an architect to ensure that the terms of his engagement are committed to paper.

3.05 If the architect writes to his client, saying that he will be delighted to work with him and setting out his fee, the letter could well constitute the offer. If the client replies agreeing to the terms, that letter constitutes the acceptance and the two letters form the contract. If the client does not reply but the architect carries on with his work with the knowledge and acquiescence of the client, there could be an acceptance of the offer by conduct. If, however, there is prolonged correspondence about the terms or if one party has indicated that not everything is agreed, it could be difficult to ascertain whether there is a finally concluded contract or not.

3.06 Secondly, if there is a concluded contract, the next question is whether it includes a commitment to give a warranty. The point is that once the contract has been concluded, the client cannot legally impose a further term into that contract, for example that warranties be provided, without the architect's consent. It is not uncommon for the architect to be sent, some time into the job, a formidable package of contract documents for his approval, and for warranties to be mentioned for the first time in those documents. In theory, if not in practice, once the architect has a concluded contract with no reference to warranties, he can refuse to countenance warranties at a later stage.

3.07 If there is a commitment to provide a warranty, the terms of the warranty which the architect has agreed to give must be certain, or the obligation may not be enforceable. If, therefore, the appointment provides that: *The Consultant agrees that he will execute a deed in favour of any party lending finance for the Development or acquiring any freehold or leasehold interest in the Development in such form as such party may reasonably require,* there may no binding obligation to give a warranty, because the terms of the warranty are too uncertain. Similarly, an agreement to provide a warranty *in a form to be agreed between the Client and the Architect* may be unenforceable, since an agreement to agree is not an enforceable contract.

3.08 Again, if there is a commitment to give a warranty, the architect will want to check that the obligation extends to the proposed beneficiary. If, say, he has undertaken to give a warranty to the first tenant of the whole or a substantial part of a development which comprises a twelve-storey office block, he is not obliged to give a warranty to a tenant taking one floor.

3.09 Thirdly, in answer to the last question, the architect should check that the warranty which he has been sent is in the same form as the one he has agreed to give, in all material respects. The contract of appointment will often include something like this: *The Consultant agrees that, within 14 days of receipt of a request to do so from the Client, he will execute a deed in favour of any party acquiring the Development in the form set out in the Schedule hereto.* If the architect finds that the warranty is not in the form set out in the schedule, then legally he can refuse to execute it.

When the obligation arises

3.10 Generally, nowadays, well-advised clients will ensure that all those from whom they will require warranties (consultants, contractors and sub-contractors) are committed to give them when requested. The client may plan to sell the project at practical completion, or he may intend to retain it while anticipating that he may wish to sell at a later date. The sale could therefore take place, and the obligation to give a warranty to a purchaser could arise at any time. If no time limit is imposed on the obligation, none is implied.

3.11 For instance, an architect may agree in a deed of appointment to give a warranty to the first purchaser of the development, but his client might not sell until fifteen years after completion. The architect's obligation is to give a warranty to that first purchaser. The limitation period will not have expired, because the period is the time within which proceedings have to be commenced for breach of contract, not the time within which the services have to be undertaken. The period does not begin to run until the breach of contract (ie the negligent or wrongful act) has been committed. Thus, if in year fifteen the architect refuses to give the warranty, the client would have twelve years (assuming the appointment was by deed) to sue him for that breach of contract.

3.12 This is an extreme example, and the client might have difficulty in proving that he has suffered loss as a result of the breach if the sale takes place so long after completion. However, as a precaution, the obligation to provide the warranty could be limited in time, for example, *to any party acquiring the Client's interest in the Development within a period of ten years from the date of practical completion of the Development as certified under the building contract.*

Time limits under warranties

3.13   In addition, it is important that the question of limitation should be addressed in the warranty itself. The limitation period cannot start to run until the warranty is given. There can be no breach of contract until the warranty has been executed, because there can be no breach when there is no contract. If (for example, because of negligent design) the architect is in breach as soon as the warranty is executed, the cause of action will arise and the limitation period will begin to run, at that time. If, therefore, in the example above, the architect is asked to give a warranty in year nine – and there is no express limitation period in the warranty – the period will be twelve years (assuming the warranty is a deed) from the date of execution, or a total of twenty-one years from completion. By means of an express clause, the limitation period can be fixed by reference to that applicable to the appointment, or a convenient date such as practical completion (see paragraph 5.74).

3.14   Thus, going back to the example in paragraph 3.11, if an architect is asked to give a warranty fifteen years after completion, so long as it includes an appropriate limitation clause (paragraph 5.79), the warranty can be given without the architect incurring any liability because any claim under it will already be time barred.

Problems with partnerships

3.15   Architects, particularly those practising as partnerships rather than companies, need to bear in mind that warranties may not be called for until some years after completion of a project.

3.16   A partnership is not a legal entity, and it is the individual partners who have the obligation to provide the warranty. Problems may arise if some partners have retired and others have joined the partnership by the time the warranty is required. The retired partners will not wish to give a warranty at that stage and the new partners may have no obligation to do so. Where a partner has died before the request is made, his estate cannot be obliged to provide the warranty.

3.17   Firms would be well advised to give the matter some thought and make appropriate provision in their partnership deeds if need be. Retired partners, if they do give a warranty, will want to ensure that they are covered by insurance, and they should therefore make provision for this, perhaps by obtaining from the continuing partnership (if there is one) an undertaking to maintain insurance or perhaps by obtaining their own run-off cover.

4   Forms of warranty

4.01   Unfortunately, there are few generally accepted forms at present, and warranties vary enormously in nature and content. They may be drafted as letters, agreements or deeds. They may be long and complicated, or short and apparently innocuous (appearances can indeed be deceptive, and a short warranty can sometimes be more onerous than a long one). The result is that there is an entirely new aspect to the contractual process: that of drafting and negotiating non-standard forms of warranty. It occupies hours of largely unproductive time for everyone involved and does considerable disservice to the, hopefully, harmonious working relationship between client and architect. A long drawn out wrangle over the terms of warranties is not a desirable start to any building project. It can set the architect and his client at loggerheads before any work has been done on the drawing board. Anything that can be done to avoid this, including the publication of widely accepted standard forms, is to be welcomed.

4.02   Mention was made in paragraph 2.14 of the standard BPF form for a financier. Before this was published, the only printed form available was that published by the RIBA for a financier. The form now agreed with the BPF varies in some respects from the RIBA form: in particular, the assignment clause is different, and a clause dealing with the provision of other warranties has been added.

4.03   The BPF and the professional bodies are now turning their attention to a purchaser and tenant warranty. In the meantime, there are a number of forms in wide circulation, for example the tenant warranty prepared by the RIBA and used by architects insured under the RIBA scheme, the warranties used by members of the Royal Incorporation of Architects in Scotland and the warranties used by members of the architects' mutual insurance company, the Wren Insurance Association Limited.

4.04   The Joint Contracts Tribunal is currently considering a standard form of warranty for contractors. It is very much to be hoped that, sooner rather than later, their deliberations will bear fruit in the form of a standard and widely accepted warranty for contractors which will dovetail with the forms being used for consultants. In the meantime, contractors' and sub-contractors' warranties vary in content quite as much as consultants' warranties.

4.05   The majority of non-standard warranties take the form of agreements or deeds. The example below illustrates a warranty between an architect and a tenant in the form of an agreement (or simple contract, see paragraph 1.15) and the example on the following page illustrates a warranty between an architect, a purchaser and the architect's client in the form of a deed (see paragraph 1.20).

THIS AGREEMENT is made   day of   199

BETWEEN
1.   [*Insert name of architect*] of/whose registered office is situated at [*insert architect's address*] ('the Consultant') and
2.   [*Insert name of tenant*] whose registered office is situated at [*insert tenant's address*] ('the Tenant').

WHEREAS:
A.   By a contract ('the Appointment') dated [*insert date of the appointment*] and made between [*insert name of the architect's client*] ('the Client') and the Consultant, the Consultant was appointed as architect in relation to the development at [*insert address of the development*] ('the Development').

B.   The Tenant has entered into an agreement for lease ('the Agreement') with the Client dated [*insert date of the agreement*] whereby the Client has agreed to grant to the Tenant a lease of part of the Development ('the Premises') as provided in the Agreement.

IT IS HEREBY AGREED as follows:
In consideration of the sum of [*insert consideration*] now paid by the Tenant to the Consultant receipt of which the Consultant hereby acknowledges:

[*insert all the clauses required*]

Signed for and on behalf of the   Signed for and on behalf of the
Consultant by   Tenant by

THIS DEED is made   day of   199

BETWEEN

1.   [*Insert name of architect*] of/whose registered office is situated at [*insert architect's address*] ('the Firm') and

2.   [*Insert name of purchaser company*] whose registered office is situated at [*insert purchaser's address*] ('the Purchaser') and

3.   [*Insert name of architect's client*] whose registered office is situated at [*insert client's address*] ('the Client')

WHEREAS:

A.   By a contract ('the Appointment') dated [*insert date of the appointment*] and made between the Client and the Firm, the Firm was appointed as architect in relation to the development at [*insert address of the development*] ('the Development').

B.   The Purchaser has entered into an agreement ('the Purchase Agreement') with the Client for the purchase of the freehold of the Development.

C.   It is a term of the Appointment and the Purchase Agreement that the Firm enter into this Agreement with the Purchaser.

NOW THIS DEED WITNESSETH as follows:

[*insert all the clauses required*]

IN WITNESS whereof the parties hereto have executed this document as a Deed the day and year first before written

Signed by [*insert architect's name*]
in the presence of [*add signature, name, address and occupation of witness*]

[*repeat for each partner in the firm*]

Signed by [*insert name of director of purchaser company*]
and [*insert name of secretary or second director*]
for and on behalf of [*insert name of purchaser company*]

Signed by [*insert name of director of client company*]
and [*insert name of secretary or second director*]
for and on behalf of [*insert name of client company*]

5   Typical clauses in a warranty

5.01   The clauses to be found in warranties are numerous and various. Some of the most common are considered below, together with two sections that often appear at the beginning of a warranty: the definition of the parties, and the recitals.

5.02   In legal documents, the convention is to define a term when it is first used and give it an initial capital letter to avoid confusion. For example, the full name of the architectural practice will be set out at the beginning of the document followed by the words (*hereinafter referred to as 'the Firm'*) or simply (*'the Firm'*). When reading a warranty therefore, every time there is a word which begins with a capital letter (other than a proper noun, of course), there should be an earlier definition stating what that word means in that document. To take an example from an architect's terms of engagement, *Purchaser* could be defined to mean *any party acquiring any freehold or leasehold interest in the property,* ie any purchaser or tenant. (A further example is given in paragraph 5.72).

Definition of the parties

5.03   Anyone who is to be privy to the warranty (that is, be bound by or be entitled to enforce its terms) must be a party. Thus the person warranting his obligations, the 'warrantor' (say, an architect), and the person obtaining the benefit of the warranty, the 'warrantee', must both be parties. If the architect's employer, the developer, is to be bound by the terms of the warranty, or has obligations thereunder, he must also be a party (in the example on page 35, the architect's client is a party to the deed). For example, in a financier warranty, if the financier is given the right to take over the architect's appointment in certain circumstances, the developer should also be a party in order to acknowledge that right. In the BPF financier's warranty, the financier, the consultant and the developer are all parties. Another reason for the developer being a party in that instance is that he undertakes to obtain warranties for the benefit of the financier from other consultants, and maybe from the contractor also (clause 12).

Recitals

5.04   The recitals set the scene by describing the relationship between the parties, their interest in the development and such like. Typically, the recitals commence with the word 'Whereas'. Care should be taken to complete the recitals so that they accurately and fully describe the position, since they can be relevant if a problem should arise on the interpretation of the warranty. The following would usually be included: a description of the property which is the subject of the warranty (note that if a tenant, for example, is taking a lease of part of a development, it would be usual to limit the warranty to that part); a description of the parties' interests in the property; and a reference to the architect's terms of engagement.

5.05   The architect's appointment should be referred to with sufficient precision, for example, *a Deed dated ...*, or *the exchange of letters attached hereto.* Thus, the BPF financier's warranty recites: *By a contract ('the Appointment') dated ...* (insert date of appointment) *the Client has appointed the Consultants as architects/consulting structural/mechanical engineers/quantity surveyors in connection with the Development.*

Consideration clause

5.06   If the warranty is in the form of an agreement or simple contract, as opposed to a deed, consideration is required for it to be enforceable (see paragraph 1.18). A typical clause would be: *In consideration of the payment of £1 by the Financier to the Architect, the receipt of which is hereby acknowledged.*

The contractual undertaking

5.07   First and foremost, the intention of a warranty is to create a contractual obligation on the part of the architect where otherwise none would exist. A typical clause would therefore be: *The Architect warrants* [or *undertakes* or *agrees*] *that he has exercised reasonable skill and care and that he will continue to exercise reasonable skill and care ...*

5.08   Sometimes this obligation is expressed in the language of tort rather than contract, for example, *The Architect owes a duty of care to the Purchaser to exercise reasonable skill and care.* However, this can be rather confusing, as the warranty is creating an obligation in contract not confirming a duty in tort.

5.09   Secondly, the intention of the warranty is to entitle a third party (a purchaser, for example) to benefit from the obligations which the architect owes his client under the terms of engagement. Therefore if the architect is in breach of his responsibilities to his client under his contract of appointment, the purchaser can sue under the warranty, because the architect will be in breach of the warranty also. In addition, the obligations under the warranty should reflect those that the architect owes to his client. For this reason the warranty will probably refer to and reflect the terms of the appointment by continuing, for example ... *in the performance of his duties and obligations under the Appointment.*

5.10   To avoid problems in the future, if the architect should be unfortunate enough to be sued on the warranty, the terms of appointment should be clearly set down in one or at the most two documents and referred to in the warranty. If there is any doubt (for instance because the offer is set out in a letter from the architect which the client did not acknowledge, or because there is a protracted exchange of correspondence containing uncertainties and ambiguities about the terms) the safest course is for a simple form of appointment to be signed. The easiest form to use is the RIBA's printed Memorandum of Agreement, which will accommodate non-standard clauses if required. A clause can be included stating that the 'effective date' is that when the architect's services began.

5.11   It is particularly important that the terms of appointment are clear when a third party (who is, generally speaking, a 'stranger' to the dealings between the architect and his client) is given a warranty. As the architect's client will probably not be a party to any proceedings in relation to the warranty, his documents and his evidence (which could be important in establishing the terms of the appointment if they are not clearly stated) might not be available.

5.12   The beneficiary of the warranty would be well advised to ensure that he is given a copy of the architect's appointment when the warranty is signed. This can also be of benefit to the architect. For example, if the architect has undertaken a limited service, he will want the warrantee to be fully aware of this. It might therefore be a good idea to attach a copy of the appointment to the warranty, particularly if the warranty is assignable.

5.13 Sometimes, a summary of the duties or services that the architect is to undertake under his appointment is set out in the warranty, but it is neater and more accurate simply to refer to the duties under the appointment, clearly identifying the document or documents which comprise that contract of appointment.

5.14 Thirdly, the architect will not expect the warranty to impose upon him duties or obligations which are greater than those he owes to his client (who instructs and pays him) and it is as well to state this expressly. For example, *The Architect shall have no duties or obligations to the Purchaser which are greater than those he owes to the Client under the Appointment.* The wording in the BPF financier's warranty is: *The Consultant shall have no greater liability to the Company by virtue of this Àgreement than he/she would have had if the Company had been named as a joint client under the Appointment.*

5.15 Fourthly, the warranty should not impose any duties or obligations on the architect which could conflict with his duties or obligations to his client. If it does, it puts the architect in an impossible position. One example of when this could arise is where an architect employed by a design and build contractor gives a warranty to the employer. The architect will want to ensure that there is no possible conflict between his primary obligations to the design and build contractor and his collateral obligations to the employer. He might, for example, consider including a clause such as this: *Any agreement or arrangement between the Architect and the Client* (ie the design and build contractor) *in respect of the Architect's duties to the Client shall likewise bind the Employer* (ie the employer under the building contract).

5.16 In the case of provisions that are contained in both the appointment and the warranty (for example, a clause relating to deleterious materials), it is sensible for them to be in the same terms – although an architect would have no objection to the provision in the warranty being less onerous than that in the appointment.

Reasonable skill and care

5.17   In giving a warranty, an architect usually undertakes to a third
        party that he will not be negligent in undertaking his duties to
        his client. This is the effect of the words: *The Architect warrants
        that he has exercised reasonable skill and care in the performance
        of his duties and obligations under the Appointment.* This
        language results in the standard of care being the same as it
        would be in tort, assuming that there was any liability in tort.
        The obligation is not to be negligent. Prior to recent court
        decisions (see case notes, section 9), it was held by the courts
        that a duty to exercise reasonable skill and care was owed to
        certain third parties in tort. However, now that architects are
        no longer likely to be liable in tort as often, they are being
        asked to enter into contractual obligations. If they undertake a
        higher standard of care in a warranty than they ever had in
        tort, they are accepting an increased liability.

5.18   The standard required of a professional person in tort is
        reasonable skill and care judged by the standards of a
        reasonably competent person of the same profession. The
        standard is that of the reasonable average. The law does not
        require of a professional man that he be a paragon, combining
        the qualities of polymath and prophet, as Lord Justice
        Bingham put it in Eckersley v Binnie & Partners (the
        Abbeystead case). It is also the standard implied in a contract
        for professional services, such as an architect's terms of
        engagement, if the contract itself is silent on the point.

5.19   Often there is an express provision in an architect's
        appointment setting out the standard of care. For example, the
        RIBA *Architect's Appointment* provides that the architect will
        exercise reasonable skill and care in conformity with the
        normal standards of the architect's profession. There is no
        reference to diligence, although this is often added. Non-
        standard terms of engagement have become common and
        nowadays they not infrequently contain variants on the
        'reasonable skill and care' wording. These variants also appear
        in warranties – and the result can be to increase the standard of
        care expected of the architect.

5.20   One way to avoid increasing the standard of care is for it to be
        qualified by the word 'reasonable': for example, *the reasonable*

skill and care to be expected or *the skill and care to be reasonably expected.* A phrase such as *all the proper skill and care to be expected* could increase the standard. The variations on this theme are endless, and it can be argued that the difference between these phrases is minimal in practice. However, a plaintiff's lawyer would doubtless do his best to exploit such differences in court, if it would be to his advantage to do so.

5.21   The clause might continue ... *to be expected of a properly qualified and competent architect experienced in carrying out projects of a similar size, scope and complexity as the Development.* It is generally thought that this does increase the standard of care, since an ordinary architect would not necessarily have this experience. A compromise wording might perhaps be ... *to be expected of a properly qualified and competent architect having regard to the size, scope and complexity of the Development.*   .

5.22   In addition to the promise that the architect will exercise reasonable skill and care in undertaking his duties and responsibilities, sometimes a warranty includes a promise on the part of the architect that he will comply with the provisions of the contract of appointment. Depending upon the terms of his appointment, there could be problems with this. The promise to exercise reasonable skill and care reflects the obligation which the architect used to have in tort, whereas an undertaking to comply with the provisions of the contract might involve a higher standard of care, either in respect of all the obligations under that contract, or in relation to some of them. In addition, in effect it means that the architect has two masters: his client, and the party to whom he has given the warranty.

Fitness for purpose

5.23   As has been explained, the standard of care implied in a contract for professional services is that of reasonable skill and care. Fitness for purpose is a higher standard, because it is an absolute obligation to achieve a certain result. If the standard is that of reasonable skill and care, the architect will be judged according to the ordinary skill of the ordinarily competent architect. If the standard is fitness for purpose, taking such reasonable skill and care might not be sufficient. It imposes an obligation to achieve a certain result and if the architect fails in this he will be liable, regardless of fault. The only relevant question is: was the design (or whatever) fit for its purpose?

5.24 One example of the difference between the two standards is that in the case of reasonable skill and care it is a defence to show that the architect did not fall below the standard prevailing in his profession at the time when the work was undertaken. The 'state of the art' is a good defence. This is not so in the case of fitness for purpose. Thus if an architect's design complied with a code of practice published at the time, but nevertheless subsequently failed, he would probably not be negligent but he could be in breach of a fitness for purpose obligation.

5.25 A slightly lower standard, reasonable fitness for purpose, is the standard implied into contracts for the sale of goods. Generally goods must be of merchantable quality and reasonably fit for the purpose for which they are supplied (by the Sale of Goods Act 1979). A fitness for purpose obligation is also implied into a contract for the supply of goods and services, such as the design and construction of a project (by the Supply of Goods and Services Act 1982). In the absence of a contrary express term (such as that which appears in the JCT Standard Form of Building Contract with Contractor's Design, 1981 Edition (CD 81)), it has been established by case law that the standard implied in a design and build contract is that the completed project will be reasonably fit for its purpose.

5.26 If a warranty includes a fitness for purpose clause, therefore, the result is to impose a higher standard of care on the architect than is usual. Further, if the architect's appointment states that he should act with reasonable skill and care, a fitness for purpose obligation in a warranty would increase the standard of care over and above that owed to the client and increase the architect's potential liability.

5.27 It is usually easy to detect a fitness for purpose clause because those particular words are used, for example *The Architect warrants and undertakes to the Purchaser that the Development when complete will be fit and suitable for its intended purpose.* However, other wording can have much the same effect, for example *The Architect warrants and undertakes to the Purchaser that the design of the Development (insofar as the*

Architect is responsible for such design or involved in the development of the design) will in all respects meet the stated requirements of the Client.

5.28   A crucial point is that most professional indemnity insurance policies do not cover a fitness for purpose obligation. This is probably why, nowadays, such clauses are seldom seen.

Indemnities

5.29   Many professional indemnity insurance policies will also not cover liabilities arising from an indemnity. These should be easy to spot, because the word 'indemnity' is usually used. For instance: *The Consultant shall indemnify and hold harmless the Purchaser from and against any claims actions costs losses and expenses made or suffered by the Purchaser as a result of any breach by the Consultant of its warranties and undertakings under this Deed.*

5.30   An indemnity increases the scope of recoverable loss beyond that normally recoverable for a breach of contract. The precise wording of an indemnity clause determines the damages recoverable, and often such clauses are widely drawn. Moreover, the effect of an indemnity clause could be to extend the limitation period considerably. This is because the limitation period, or time limit for starting a legal action, runs from the date of the particular breach of contract against which recourse is sought. In the case of an indemnity, the breach of contract does not occur until the beneficiary incurs the loss against which he is entitled to be indemnified, ie the liability is identified. (For instance, if a purchaser under a warranty is entitled to an indemnity in respect of the cost of remedial works necessitated by the architect's negligence, the time limit runs from the date the remedial works were undertaken, not from the date when the architect was negligent.)

Preservation of tortious rights and reliance

5.31   Sometimes reference is made in a warranty to tortious rights, in an endeavour to preserve what rights the beneficiary might have in tort over and above the rights being given under the warranty.

The extent to which the beneficiary of a warranty would retain tortious rights is to some extent uncertain. *Cementation v Greater Nottingham Council* suggests that he could not obtain in tort remedies which he did not have under the warranty. In that case, an employer had a warranty from a sub-contractor, but the terms of the warranty did not cover the particular loss which the employer suffered and was seeking to recover.

5.32   A clause such as the following expressly preserves tortious rights: *This Agreement is without prejudice to any rights and remedies of the Purchaser against the Architect at common law or otherwise.* This would seem to mean in effect that the purchaser could avoid the *Cementation* problem.

5.33   Sometimes there is a clause such as the following: *The Purchaser shall be deemed to have relied upon the Architect.* The purchaser might seek to argue that the architect therefore owed him a *Hedley Byrne* type 'reliance duty' (see case notes, 9.14), although whether the courts would permit this interpretation remains to be seen. The importance of this type of duty is that if there is a breach, the purchaser would be able to recover economic loss in tort. It could well be that in the absence of such a clause the purchaser could not satisfy the requirements to establish a 'reliance duty'.

Damages recoverable ('economic and consequential loss')

5.34   If a limit on the damages recoverable is not inserted into a warranty, the architect will be taking the risk of having greater liability than he would have had in tort, even before the restrictions imposed by the recent case law. Moreover, that greater liability could be considerable.

5.35   One of the important differences between liability in contract and tort is that there are different rules as to the recovery of damages. In contract there is no limitation on the recovery of financial or economic loss *per se*. The plaintiff is entitled to damages so that, insofar as money can do it, he is placed in the same position that he would have been in had the contract been performed, subject to certain rules about the foreseeability of loss. The position in tort is different, and traditionally a distinction has been drawn between physical injury and damage to property on the one hand (which generally was recoverable) and 'economic loss' on the other (which usually was not recoverable). Although recent cases (see case notes, section 9) have considerably limited what losses are recoverable in tort, even before these decisions there were limits on the recovery of economic loss.

5.36   One problem therefore for those granting warranties is that by making available contractual remedies rather than tortious ones, the category of damages recoverable will be different, difficult to predict and potentially much greater (and, therefore, problematic to insure). Examples of pure economic loss that could be recoverable under a warranty are loss of profit, loss of interest, loss of rent and diminution in value. Such losses could easily be much greater than the cost of remedying defective work.

5.37   It is for these reasons that warranties often restrict the type of damages recoverable, in the case of an occupier or a non-occupier. This used to be expressed in wording such as: *any liability for economic and consequential losses incurred by the Purchaser, howsoever arising, is hereby expressly excluded.* The main problem with this is that it is not entirely clear what the term *economic and consequential loss* covers.

5.38   It is usual nowadays, therefore, to see more positive wording, restricting the architect's liability to the cost of remedying defects in (or damage to) the development only. For example: *The Firm's liability to the Purchaser shall be limited to the reasonable costs of remedying damage to the Development directly caused by the Firm's failure to exercise reasonable skill and care and it is hereby agreed and acknowledged that all other losses incurred by the Purchaser, howsoever arising, are expressly excluded.*

5.39   This restriction of the architect's liability under the warranty to the cost of remedying defective work only, is not applicable in the case of a financier who only has a charge over the property (see paragraph 2.12). His losses are bound to be purely economic due to the nature of his interest. On the other hand, it is applicable in the case of a fund who is purchasing the property. This is why the difference between a lender who is taking a charge over the development and one who is purchasing it, is important.

Deleterious materials

5.40 Subject to anything contained in his contract of appointment, the architect has a duty to take reasonable skill and care in all the services he undertakes pursuant to that appointment. It is not, therefore, essential to spell out his obligations in relation to any particular duty, for example that of compiling the specification. Nevertheless, it has become common to refer to deleterious materials specifically.

5.41 Sometimes, the standard of care is 'reasonable skill and care'. For example, the clause in the BPF financier's warranty reads as follows: *The Consultant further warrants that he/she has exercised and will continue to exercise reasonable skill and care to see that unless authorised by the Client none of the following has been or will be specified by the Consultant for use in the construction of those parts of the Development to which the Appointment relates.* It will be seen that the obligation is limited to specification *by the Consultant* himself and *to those parts of the Development to which the Appointment relates.*

5.42 On occasion, the duty is expressed to be absolute, for example: *The Architect undertakes that he has not and will not specify any of the following for use.* In this case, it would be no defence for the architect to show that he had unwittingly, and not negligently, specified one of the listed materials. For this reason, he might prefer to agree *not knowingly to specify.*

5.43 In both the examples above, the obligation is limited to specifying, and there is no reference to inspection duties. An example that included inspection would be ... *and will ensure that they are not used.* The trouble with this, so far as the architect is concerned, is that he is not in a position to determine precisely what is used on site, as his assessment of the contractor's workmanship is usually limited to periodic inspection, which might be visiting about once a week on average. Any obligation in relation to inspection should therefore be looked at critically.

5.44 The lists themselves vary enormously. Sometimes they include items which are not deleterious in the true sense, but are materials which the developer or warrantee would not like to see used in his development (for example tropical hardwoods). Some materials may be deleterious in some circumstances but not in others (for example lead, which is now considered deleterious if used extensively in drinking water pipes but is quite acceptable if used in flashings). The architect is well advised to check every list he sees – it could have been drafted by someone who has no idea what any of the materials are.

5.45 Care should also be taken with general sweep-up provisions, for example *any other materials generally known to be deleterious*. This is widely drawn and the following is more precise: *any other materials generally known by the architects' profession at the time of specification to be deleterious*. There could however be considerable argument in years to come, as to what was generally known at any particular time.

5.46 If there is a deleterious materials clause in the appointment, it is preferable that the clause in the warranty is in the same terms. It certainly should not be in conflicting terms.

Insurance clause

5.47 The beneficiaries of warranties will generally be relying on the architect having professional indemnity insurance in the event that they have a sizeable claim. To protect their position therefore, it has become common for an insurance clause to be included in most warranties.

5.48 As an example, the clause in the BPF financier's warranty reads as follows: *The Consultant shall maintain professional indemnity insurance in the amount of not less than ... pounds for any one occurrence or series of occurrences arising out of any one event for a period of ... years from the date of practical completion of the Development for the purposes of the Building Contract provided always that such insurance is available in the market at commercially reasonable rates. The Consultant shall immediately inform the Company if such insurance ceases to be available at commercially reasonable rates. As and when he/she is reasonably requested by the Company ... the Consultant shall produce for inspection documentary evidence that his/her professional indemnity insurance is being maintained.*

5.49   It is not clear how this clause could be enforced in practice. A remedy in damages may be difficult to pursue, since if the beneficiary of the warranty sues for breach of the clause in circumstances where he has no other claim, it is not certain what damages he would recover (and there would appear to be no case on the point). If he does have a substantive claim, he can only recover from the architect in any event, and the damages he would claim for breach of the insurance clause would be the same as his damages in respect of the claim.

5.50   The architect will probably want some escape from the obligation to maintain insurance in the event that he finds it becomes prohibitively expensive or he simply cannot afford it. This can be done by qualifying the obligation by the *reasonable commercial rates* formula from the BPF financier's warranty referred to above. An alternative is for the obligation to be expressed in terms of *will make reasonable endeavours to maintain*. The advantage of this so far as the architect is concerned is that insurance might be available at a reasonable commercial rate but his financial position might be such that, using reasonable endeavours, he could not afford to maintain cover. Not infrequently, the term used is *best endeavours*. This would require the architect to use a greater degree of endeavour, as the wording implies.

5.51   If a period for the maintenance of insurance is stated, it should be the same as (or shorter than) the limitation period under the warranty (see paragraph 5.74).

Copyright, licences and provision of drawings

5.52   A detailed explanation of the law of copyright is outside the scope of this book, but it is common for clauses dealing with copyright and related matters to appear in warranties, and one or two basic points follow.

5.53   First, the relevant provisions that appear in the architect's appointment must be looked at alongside those in the warranty to ensure that there is no conflict. Unless there is some provision to the contrary in the appointment, the architect has copyright in his own work. He can therefore grant licences. However if, as occasionally happens, the architect has given the copyright to his client, he has no power to grant licences under the warranty.

5.54   Secondly, the architect may want to give some thought to the extent of the licence he is granting. The wording in the BPF financier's warranty is ... *a licence to copy and use such drawings and other documents and to reproduce the designs contained in them for any purpose related to the Development including, but without limitation, the construction, completion, maintenance, letting, promotion, advertisement, reinstatement and repair of the Development.*

5.55   Two useful sentences follow, first: *The Company* [the financier] *and its appointee shall have a licence to copy and use such drawings and other documents for the extension of the Development but such use shall not include a licence to reproduce the designs contained in them for any extension of the Development.* Second: *The Firm* [the architect] *shall not be liable for any such use by the Company or its appointee of any drawings and other documents for any purpose other than that for which the same were prepared and provided by the Firm.*

5.56   Thirdly, a clause requiring the architect to provide copies of drawings and other documents may also appear in the warranty. The architect will want to consider the practical implications of accepting such a commitment. For example, who will pay the copying charges or any other associated costs? How long will the commitment last and will it be practical to continue to make the copies available? If no time limit is placed on the obligation, the architect can be asked for the drawings or documents at any time. He might therefore prefer a clause such as this: *The Consultant agrees on request at any time within a period of ten years from practical completion to give the Purchaser access to and copies of any drawings* [or documents] *in his possession relating to the Development, upon payment of his reasonable costs.*

Assignment

5.57   On an assignment the rights (benefits) or obligations (burdens) under a contract – which could be a warranty – are transferred by one of the parties to a third party. No new contract is created (as in the case of novation, see paragraph 5.84) but the rights or obligations are passed from the original contracting party to the third party. The law in this area is difficult for lawyers, let alone architects, to comprehend fully.

BENEFITS AND BURDENS

5.58   In the case of an architect's appointment, the benefit to the client is the architectural services and the burden is the obligation to pay for them. As far as the architect is concerned, the benefit is the fee and the burden is the obligation to perform the services. In the case of a warranty, to the warrantee (for example, a purchaser) the benefit is the architect's contractual undertaking. There may be no burden at all, save perhaps for the payment of the consideration, copying charges for drawings and the like, and (where there are step-in rights, see paragraph 5.81) payment of the architect's fees in certain circumstances. For the architect the burden is the obligation owed to the purchaser, while the benefit is, on the face of it, small indeed.

5.59   The benefit of a contract is generally assignable without consent. Therefore (subject to what is said in the following paragraph) a purchaser who has a warranty could pass on the benefit of the architect's undertaking to a subsequent purchaser. On the other hand, the burden can only be assigned if there is an express right contained in the contract itself, or the architect consents to an assignment.

5.60   One exception to the rule that the benefit can be assigned is what is described as a personal contract (for instance, the right to employ a person under a contract of employment is not assignable). The question therefore is whether a warranty would be regarded as a personal contract or not, and there is no authority on the point. Lawyers disagree, although the majority view appears to be that warranties are not personal contracts. Having said that, there might be circumstances rendering a particular warranty personal.

5.61   This means that if there is no reference in the warranty to assignment (or rights being conferred on successors in title, see paragraph 5.72), there is some doubt whether or not the benefits are assignable, although probably in most instances they are. Warranties are generally only offered to the first purchaser or tenant of a development, and it will therefore be of concern to a subsequent purchaser or tenant (and indeed to the original purchaser or tenant who wants to sell his interest) whether the benefit of the warranty can be passed on. Due to this uncertainty, it is common to see a clause in a warranty clearly stating whether it may be assigned or not.

5.62   An example of a clause prohibiting assignment would be: *This Agreement is personal to the parties and may not be assigned.* If, on the other hand, the warranty provides for assignment, it may do so in a variety of different terms, and to understand them it is necessary to look briefly at the law relating to assignment.

LEGAL AND EQUITABLE ASSIGNMENT

5.63   The law recognises two broad categories of assignment: 'legal' assignments and 'equitable' assignments. The distinction between the two has arisen because of the way in which English law has developed. Their present significance is partly to do with procedural technicalities: if there has been a legal assignment then the assignee (ie the party acquiring the benefit of the warranty) can sue under the warranty in his own name, whereas if there has been an equitable assignment, matters are not so straightforward and the assignor should be a party to the action (as plaintiff, if he agrees, or as defendant if he does not). As will be seen, there are also other differences.

5.64   A legal assignment is one which complies with section 136 of the Law of Property Act 1925. Taking the example of a warranty given by an architect to a first purchaser which is to be assigned to the second purchaser, the section requires that the assignment must be in writing under the hand of the first purchaser (the assignor) and that express written notice of the assignment must be given to the architect by the second purchaser (the assignee). The notice can be given at any time up to the issue of a writ. It must also be an absolute assignment, that is, not by way of charge only, nor an assignment of part only of the benefit of the warranty. Take as an example a first purchaser of a development comprising two buildings, who has one warranty. If he sells one of the buildings, he could not make a legal assignment of his rights under the warranty in connection with that building, while retaining his rights in connection with the other building. In addition, a legal assignment cannot be qualified by conditions.

5.65   Any valid assignment which does not satisfy section 136 will be an equitable assignment. For example, if in the case above the first purchaser fails to give notice to the architect, the transaction may nevertheless be valid as an equitable assignment. An equitable assignment can be by way of charge only, or be of part of a warranty.

5.66   An example of a clause providing for legal assignment is: *This Agreement may be assigned by way of absolute legal assignment to a party acquiring the Purchaser's entire interest in the development, but not otherwise.*

5.67   There is no reference to consent in the example above, although it is not uncommon to see the following: ... *may be assigned without the Architect's consent.* Sometimes the clause reads: ... *with the Architect's consent, which shall not be unreasonably withheld*, which is different from *with the Architect's consent.* The difference is important. If there is no qualification on the consent, then the firm can consent or not, entirely at its will or whim (although commercial pressures may be brought to bear). However, if consent is not to be unreasonably withheld, the firm would have to be cautious in refusing consent. There would have to be a reason, and what would constitute a sufficiently good reason would depend upon the circumstances. It would be prudent to assume that consent would have to be given in most cases.

5.68   The BPF financier's warranty includes the following assignment clause: *This Agreement may be assigned by the Company by way of absolute legal assignment to another company providing finance or re-finance in connection with the Development without the consent of the Client or the Firm being required and such assignment shall be effective upon written notice thereof being given to the Client and to the Firm.*

5.69   The reference in the clause above is to absolute legal assignment, and to another company as described. It is understood to be intended (by the RIBA, in any event) that the assignment permitted is to another financier only, and not to a financing or funding purchaser, although this may not be clear from the drafting. It will also be noted that there is no time limit within which the assignment may take place. However, *the Development* is defined as the carrying out of the works (as set out) at the specified address, which limits the assignee to a party lending money for the purpose of carrying out the project as so defined.

5.70   If a clause provides for legal assignment *but not otherwise* then equitable assignment is prohibited. A clause such as the following permits legal and equitable assignment: *This Agreement may be freely assigned.*

5.71   Alternatively, a clause might attempt to limit the number of assignments, for example: *This Agreement may be assigned once to a party acquiring the Purchaser's entire interest in the Project.* Arguably, there is a problem with this, in that the subsequent purchaser, to whom the warranty is assigned, steps into the shoes of the first purchaser, and acquires the same rights that he had, including the right to assign the warranty once. For this reason, the following might be preferable: *This Agreement may be assigned with the consent of the Architect, such consent not to be withheld in the case of the first party acquiring the Purchaser's entire interest.*

5.72   The definition of the parties may in effect give an express right of assignment. For example, where a warranty is given to *City Centre Properties Ltd of ... (hereinafter referred to as 'the Purchaser' which expression shall include its successors in title and assigns)* it is clearly envisaged that the purchaser can assign the warranty.

WHAT IS BEING ASSIGNED?

5.73   Under a warranty, the party to whom it is given has the right to sue if the architect is in breach, and to recover damages. Following an assignment, the new beneficiary of a warranty cannot recover more than the original beneficiary could have recovered. This is not an easy area of law. It would appear that the new beneficiary will be able to recover consequential losses of the same type as the original beneficiary would have suffered. If, however, there is a change of use upon the assignment, and the new beneficiary suffers a greater loss than his predecessor would have done, then he cannot recover that loss. These problems do not arise if the warranty restricts the type of losses recoverable to remedial works only (see paragraphs 5.34–5.38).

Limitation

5.74   It is now not uncommon for architects' terms of engagement to be in the form of deeds rather than simple contracts, resulting in an extension of the limitation period from six years from the date of breach of contract to twelve. Those seeking warranties also often ask that they are in the form of deeds. They are then effective without the need for consideration. The unfortunate result, from the architect's point of view, is that contractual liability subsists for twice as long as it would if the warranty was in the form of a simple contract. On the other hand, it could be argued that twelve years brings the limitation period nearer to what it would be in tort if a duty were owed, ie six years from the date when damage occurred, which can be some time after completion, plus the additional time limit afforded by the Latent Damage Act 1986 of three years from discoverability. (There is a cut-off date of fifteen years from breach of contract, but this is not absolute.)

5.75   The present law of limitation is not without its difficulties. It has been criticised for being both complicated and uncertain, for example in *Professional Liability: Report of the Study Teams* published by the Department of Trade and Industry in April 1989, of which the Report of the Construction Professionals Study Team (chaired by Professor Donald Bishop) formed part. In that report it was proposed that the Limitation Acts be amended to provide for a fixed period of ten years from practical completion or effective occupation, in tort and contract (both simple contracts and deeds).

5.76   The limitation period under a contract can be varied by agreement. It is not unusual therefore to see a warranty in the form of a deed with an express limitation period limiting liability to six years, or perhaps eight, nine or ten years.

5.77   In particular, it has become quite common to see an express limitation period of ten years from practical completion. This has the advantage of certainty. Ten years from practical completion is also the period recommended in the report referred to in paragraph 5.75. If the appointment is by way of deed, the limitation period will be twelve years from the date of the relevant breach of contract, and this is not necessarily twelve years from practical completion. For example, if the negligence which caused the plaintiff's loss was advice given about ground conditions, that advice may have been given several years before practical completion. On the other hand, if the negligence was the issuing of the final certificate, that would be when the twelve years would begin to run. It is for this reason that, even in contract, the limitation period can be uncertain. Ten years from practical completion could be a longer or shorter period than twelve years from breach of contract. An express clause can therefore provide either a fixed period or a maximum period (say ten years from practical completion) rather than an uncertain period (twelve years from the date of breach of contract).

5.78   As noted in paragraph 3.13, it is important to include a limitation clause in a warranty, particularly if the warranty is not executed until some time after the development is complete.

5.79   Examples of limitation clauses are: *The limitation period applicable to this Agreement shall be no longer than x years from the date of practical completion*; or, *The Consultant shall have no liability under this Agreement after the expiration of x years from the date of practical completion.*

5.80   An alternative approach is to say that the architect's duties, obligations or liabilities are *no greater than and of no longer duration than* those under the appointment (see paragraph 5.14). This means that if the appointment is by way of deed, the limitation period will be twelve years from the date of breach of contract, or in the case of a simple contract, six years. However, there could be an argument that the words are not clear enough to alter the limitation period and therefore it might be as well to include an express limitation clause.

Novation and step-in rights

5.81   Where a financier has lent money for the construction of a development, he will be concerned to protect his loan in the event of the developer getting into financial difficulties or defaulting on the loan repayments. The same is true of a forward-funding purchaser, and the comments below apply to any party lending finance for the carrying out of the project. The financial arrangements between a developer and financier vary enormously and generally the architect will not be privy to them. He is, though, likely to be asked to give a warranty to a financier, who will want to have direct recourse to the architect as well as to the other members of the design team and the contractor.

5.82   If the developer defaults, the financier may need to sell the development to recoup his loan and accrued interest. However, selling an incomplete development could be difficult or might raise insufficient funds and therefore the financier will want to make arrangements for the development to be completed before selling it. To enable him to do this, he will include in his warranty the right to take over the architect's appointment in certain circumstances by step-in rights or a right to novate. Similar provisions will appear in the warranties given by the other consultants and the building contractor.

5.83   These rights to step in or novate are mechanisms by which a financier can take over the role of the architect's client, usually during the course of construction. Sometimes the right to take over is expressed as an agreement that the architect's appointment will be novated to the financier. Frequently, however, the term novation is not used (or the ingredients for a novation agreement are not set out) but a procedure whereby the financier can step into the shoes of the architect's client is described. 'Step-in rights' is not a recognised legal term and in practice the exercise of these rights could be effected by assignment or novation of the architect's appointment. However, the legal niceties will not concern the architect – so long as, if the need arises, the takeover of the project by the financier goes smoothly and the architect recovers his fees.

5.84   In the case of novation, the original contract between the developer and the architect will cease to have effect, and (by agreement of all the parties, ie the developer, architect and financier) a new contract will be entered into between the architect and the financier, usually on the same terms as the original appointment. This is effected by a 'novation agreement' to which the developer, architect and financier will all be parties. It is not uncommon for a document to be described as a 'novation agreement' but for it to provide for something other than a strict novation in legal terms. Since such an arrangement is arrived at with the agreement of all parties, this is not a problem. Novation should be contrasted with assignment (see paragraph 5.57). For example, if a developer assigns an architect's appointment to a financier, the architect would not need to be a party to the assignment, and the original appointment would be passed on rather than a new one created.

5.85 The terms of the various contracts concerned will determine what types of rights arise and in what circumstances. The funding agreement, the architect's appointment and the financier's warranty will all be relevant. Since only the parties to a contract are bound by its terms, the operation of the provisions in the various different contracts should be co-ordinated at the drafting stage.

5.86 There are two circumstances for which the financier may be given step-in or novation rights. The first situation is where the developer is in default under the funding agreement, typically for failure to meet interest payments on the monies borrowed. In this case the right will normally arise upon the financier giving the architect notice that the funding agreement has been terminated. See, for example, clause 5 of the BPF financier's warranty, which reads: *The Firm agrees that, in the event of the termination of the Finance Agreement by the Company, the Firm will, if so required by notice in writing given by the Company ... accept the instructions of the Company or its appointee to the exclusion of the Client in respect of the Development upon the terms and conditions of the Appointment.*

5.87 When he receives that type of notice, the architect needs to ensure that he is entitled and obliged to treat the financier as his client, since otherwise he could be in breach of his appointment. Thus, for example, clause 5 referred to above continues: *The Client acknowledges that the Firm shall be entitled to rely on a notice given to the Firm by the Company under this Clause 5 as conclusive evidence for the purposes of this Agreement of the termination of the Finance Agreement by the Company.*

5.88   The second situation is where the developer is in such serious
        default under the architect's appointment that the architect has
        a right to determine his contract. In this eventuality the rights
        will arise by the architect giving the financier notice of his
        intention to terminate his appointment. During the notice
        period the financier can decide whether to exercise his rights to
        become the architect's employer or not.

5.89   Clause 6 of the BPF financier's warranty thus provides: *The
        Firm further agrees that it will not without first giving the
        Company not less than twenty one days' notice in writing exercise
        any right it may have to terminate the Appointment or to treat
        the same as having been repudiated by the Client or to discontinue
        the performance of any duties to be performed by the Firm
        pursuant thereto. The Firm's right to terminate the Appointment
        with the Client or treat the same as having been repudiated or
        discontinue performance shall cease if, within such period of
        notice ... the Company shall give notice in writing to the Firm
        requiring the Firm to accept the instructions of the Company or
        its appointee to the exclusion of the Client in respect of the
        Development upon the terms and conditions of the Appointment.*

5.90   The developer should be a party to the warranty, so that he is
        bound by these provisions. It is also wise to include a clause
        such as the following (from the BPF financier's warranty): *The
        Client has agreed to be a party to this Agreement ... for
        acknowledging that the Firm shall not be in breach of the
        Appointment by complying with the obligations imposed on it by
        Clauses 5 and 6.*

5.91   Clauses 5 and 6 from the BPF financier's warranty describe a
        machinery for the financier to step into the shoes of the
        architect's client. An example of a clause specifically providing
        for novation would be: *The Architect agrees not to exercise any
        right to terminate the Appointment without first giving the Fund
        fourteen days' notice in writing. The Fund may, following receipt
        of such notice, require the Architect to enter into a novation
        agreement with the Fund in the form attached to this Deed.*

5.92   Since the financier will not be exercising these rights unless the
        developer is in default in one way or another, there is a good
        chance that the architect will at that stage have fees owing to
        him. He will therefore want to ensure if he can that not only

does the financier undertake to pay the fees for any further work, but that he pays any outstanding fees. For example, Clause 5 of the BPF financier's warranty provides that: *It shall be a condition of any notice given by the Company under Clause 5 or 6 that the Company or its appointee accepts liability for payment of the fees payable to the Firm under the Appointment including payment of any fees outstanding at the date of such notice.* It is a matter for negotiation, but not all financiers are happy to pay outstanding fees, because they might have advanced them to the developer as part of his loan and they would not want to pay them twice. Often, in such a situation, the developer will not be worth suing.

5.93   As a practical point, if the architect is in any difficulty with his original client at the time that the financier takes over, it would be as well to advise the financier of this at an early stage. An example would be if the client had failed to give the architect proper instructions, and this had delayed the building contract. The financier will in any event probably be taking over the building contract as well and he will rely on the architect and other members of the design team for information about the position under that contract.

5.94   Occasionally there is no provision for step-in rights or novation in the financier's warranty, but the matter is addressed in the architect's contract of appointment instead. This can be done by providing in the appointment itself that it can be novated to the financier at any time. The appropriate clause is likely to appear in the section dealing with assignment. Again, the architect will want to consider his position regarding fees.

Other warranties

5.95   The problem of joint liability and other warranties is a complex subject and is dealt with in the following section. Whenever an architect gives a warranty, he would be well advised to ensure that the problems created by joint liability are addressed.

6 Joint liability and the need for other warranties

6.01   Joint and several liability, in the context of warranties, causes a particular problem. If, when the architect gives a warranty, those with whom he is jointly liable in respect of the same damage (and who have a contractual relationship with the employer as the architect does) do not also give warranties, then the architect pays all the losses that result if he is sued under the warranty. This is because he is unable to obtain from the others the contribution that he would be able to recover if they were both sued by the employer.

6.02   The problem can arise whenever participants in the design and construction team are partly liable in respect of the same damage. The most obvious example is where the architect is negligent in failing to discover the contractor's bad workmanship. The damage that results from the contractor's bad workmanship and the architect's negligent inspection is the same: the cost of putting the defects right. Each is partly liable for the damage, and each is in breach of his contract – in the contractor's case the building contract, and in the architect's case the appointment. The employer is able, in English law, to recover 100% of the cost of remedial works from either the contractor or the architect (either of whom can then seek a contribution from the other).

6.03   The difficulty arises because of the way in which English law works and the easiest way to understand it is by taking an example. First of all it is necessary to consider the relationship between the developer, his architect and the contractor, as well as the architect's position under the appointment, before turning to look at the situation when warranties have been executed.

The position under the appointment

6.04   Assume that a building owner finds that there are a number of defects in his building, an office block. (If it had been a dwelling the Defective Premises Act 1972 would apply, and the position would be different in that it would be necessary to consider the liability of the architect and contractor under that Act as well as in contract.) The expert evidence is that all the defects are problems of bad workmanship. The employer goes to court, the judge agrees with his expert evidence, and the contractor is therefore found liable because he is in breach of the building contract. His liability is for the total cost of remedial works necessitated by his breach of contract, let us say £150,000.

6.05   Assume that the employer also sues the architect whom he engaged in respect of the same defects. The judge decides that, in relation to some of the defects, the architect was not negligent in the course of his inspections on site. The cost of putting right those defects is £50,000. However, the judge goes on to decide that in relation to the remaining defects the architect was negligent. The architect is therefore in breach of his contract to the employer and is responsible for the cost of remedying defects caused by his negligence, ie £100,000.

6.06   Both the contractor and the architect are liable to the employer for the damages that flow from their respective breaches of contract. In the case of the contractor this is £150,000; in the case of the architect £100,000. For two thirds of the cost of remedial works therefore, both the contractor and the architect are liable in respect of the same damage. They are both 100% liable to the employer for those remedial costs of £100,000.

6.07   However, the employer cannot recover twice. If they both have judgment entered against them, the contractor or the architect can ask the court to apportion the liability between them under the Civil Liability (Contribution) Act 1978. Section 1(1) states that *any person liable in respect of any damage suffered by another person may recover contribution from any other person liable in respect of the same damage (whether jointly with him or otherwise)*. If the employer sued only one of the defendants, say the contractor, then the contractor could join the architect as a third party to that action, claiming contribution under the Act.

6.08   Say that the Court makes an apportionment of 75% to the contractor and 25% to the architect. The net result of this is that the contractor has to pay £50,000 (for which he alone is liable) plus £75,000 (his apportioned share), and the architect has to pay £25,000 (his share). Nevertheless, if he chooses, the employer can still enforce his judgment for £100,000 in full against either the contractor or the architect. If he enforces against the architect who then pays the employer £100,000, the architect can seek a contribution of £75,000 from the contractor.

6.09 However, if the contractor has gone into liquidation and therefore cannot pay, the employer has recovered his £100,000 from the architect, but the architect cannot obtain his contribution. If either the architect or contractor cannot pay his share, the other one is responsible for paying the whole £100,000.

The position when warranties are executed

6.10 Turning to the position when warranties are executed, assume that the employer sold the building to a purchaser and it is the purchaser who suffers the loss. If he has obtained warranties from both the contractor and the architect the result is the same as in the example above. If both the contractor and the architect are good for the money, the purchaser recovers £150,000 of which the contractor will contribute £125,000 (£50,000 plus £75,000) and the architect £25,000. If the contractor is unable to pay, the purchaser receives £100,000 from the architect; if the architect is unable to pay, he recovers £150,000 from the contractor.

6.11 If the purchaser has only obtained a warranty from the architect, he will not be able to recover anything from the contractor. He will not be able to recover the £50,000 or any part of the £100,000 from him because he has no contract with the contractor. (It is assumed that there is no liability in tort.)

6.12 However, the purchaser will be able to recover £100,000 from the architect under his warranty. The problem for the hapless architect who signed the warranty is that he cannot obtain a contribution from the contractor under the 1978 Act. The architect and the contractor are no longer liable in respect of the same damage (ie the damage suffered by the purchaser). The contractor has no liability to the purchaser in contract or tort, so that he and the architect are not joint contract breakers or joint tortfeasors and the contractor does not owe the architect a duty in tort. In this situation, the purchaser is worse off by £50,000, and the architect is worse off by £75,000. Compare this with the case where the contractor also gave a warranty, when the purchaser would be able to recover £150,000 in full – £125,000 from the contractor and £25,000 from the architect.

6.13   It can therefore be seen that it is important to those giving warranties that any other party with whom they might be jointly liable also gives a warranty. In the example above it is the difference between the architect paying £25,000 and £100,000.

Who could be jointly liable?

6.14   The example of an architect inspecting the contractor's workmanship was given in paragraph 6.02, but the architect (because of his co-ordinating role) could be jointly liable with anyone else undertaking design, whether a consultant or sub-contractor. For example, under his terms of engagement the architect generally co-ordinates and integrates the structural engineer's design into the overall design, and some errors made by the engineer will be of the kind that should be picked up by a reasonably competent architect. Therefore if the architect fails to do this he is negligent, and the damages that result from the negligence of the engineer and the architect in that situation will often be the same. If the error was made not by the structural engineer but by a design sub-contractor whose design the architect was co-ordinating and integrating, the architect would be jointly liable with that sub-contractor.

6.15   Who could be jointly liable with the architect will depend to some extent upon the contractual relationships. In the case of a traditional form of building contract where the architect is leader of the design team, this could be anyone else responsible for design, and the contractor whose work he inspects; for the contractor it could be anyone who inspects his work, and sub-contractors. In other methods of building procurement the net could be wider. For example, take a construction management contract, where the trade contractors are employed direct by the employer and are not sub-contracted to the construction manager (see paragraph 2.06). Within the works packages, the trade contractors undertake on-site works, which the architect inspects. The trade contractors might also undertake design which – assuming that he is undertaking the full normal service – the architect coordinates. The architect could therefore be jointly liable with any trade contractor.

Criticism of the present law

6.16   The law relating to joint liability has been criticised, in particular in the Report of the Construction Professional Study Team which formed part of *Professional Liability: Report of the Study Teams*, referred to in paragraph 5.75. The report's recommendations included (on page 118):

'The Study Team recommends that serious consideration be given to the alteration of the law in commercial transactions, not involving personal injury, where the plaintiff's claim exceeds, say, £50,000. In such cases, a defendant whose actions are partly the cause of damage to the plaintiff, but such actions were not carried out jointly with another defendant, should be responsible to the plaintiff only for damages equivalent to that part of the plaintiff's loss fairly attributable to his or her breach. ... This recommendation is strongly supported by the professional institutions and consultants' associations. The British Property Federation accepts that the current law can be unfair to consultants. Clearly, this recommendation raises issues of public policy.'

The 'network of contracts'

6.17   Because of the number of warranties now being executed, there is an increased risk that the architect, or anyone else who gives warranties, will be liable for an unfair proportion of loss.

6.18   If the 'network of contracts' is not reproduced by warranties being given by every party having responsibility for the design and construction, those who have executed warranties carry the risk of bearing an unfair proportion of the damages resulting from their breach of contract. This is because they will not be able to claim a contribution from others jointly liable with them. The party obtaining the warranty will not suffer, but the party giving it will. By 'network of contracts' is meant all those contractual relationships which come into existence when an employer undertakes a development, entering into contracts with, for example, a design team and a main contractor, who employs sub-contractors, from some of whom the employer obtains direct warranties. (See section 2 for a discussion on who might be asked to give warranties).

6.19   Under his appointment, the problem for the architect is that if any party with whom he is found jointly liable in respect of the same damage cannot pay his apportioned share, the architect bears the whole loss. In other words, the architect is bearing the risk of the insolvency of the others jointly liable with him. (They, of course, bear the risk of his insolvency.)

6.20   In the context of the architect giving a warranty, there are two problems. The first problem is ensuring that any others who might be jointly liable also give warranties, and the second problem is the insolvency of those others.

Possible solutions

6.21   There is no simple solution to the problem of joint liability in the context of warranties. Some solutions tackle the first problem referred to in the previous paragraph but not the second. This is one area in particular where the practice is changing.

6.22   One solution, favoured by those giving warranties, was a 'condition precedent' clause, for instance: *This Agreement shall only take effect where all other consultants and contractors employed by the Client have given warranties to the Purchaser in connection with the Development* ... The effect was that the architect had no liability at all (even where he was not jointly liable with another) unless other warranties had been obtained. This solved the first problem but not the second. It was not liked by those obtaining warranties, and is now little used.

6.23   An alternative solution is for the architect to obtain a contractual commitment that other warranties will be obtained. The commitment can be made by his client (either in the terms of appointment, in the warranty or in a side letter of some kind) or by the beneficiary of the warranty. Again this solution addresses the first problem but not the second. It may not solve the first problem, because it is doubtful what remedy the architect would have against his client or the beneficiary if they did not obtain the other warranties and were therefore in breach of contract. For example, if the architect were sued under the warranty for negligent inspection but the contractor had not given a warranty, the architect would argue that the damages that he had suffered would be the contribution he could have obtained from the contractor if he had given a warranty. In the example in paragraphs 6.04 to 6.13 above, his loss would be £75,000. Could he recover that sum from the client or beneficiary? The answer is not clear.

6.24   In the BPF financier's warranty there is a provision that the employer (not the financier) undertakes to obtain other warranties. Clause 12 reads: *The Client undertakes to the Firm that warranty agreements in the Model Form CoWa/F published by the British Property Federation* [ie the BPF financier's warranty] *or in substantially similar form have been or will be entered into between* [insert names and/or descriptions of other parties required to sign warranty agreements] *on the one hand and the Company* [the financier] *on the other.*

6.25   It is not at all certain that this is effective, for the reason set out above. In addition, however, the financier's warranty will almost certainly not be enforced unless the client is in some financial difficulty, since it is only then that the financier suffers loss as a result of the client defaulting on the funding agreement. In that situation it would probably not be worthwhile for the architect to pursue the client in any event.

6.26   The reference in clause 12 above is to the other warranties being in the form of the BPF financier's warranty, or substantially similar form. One difficulty is that there is at present no generally accepted form of warranty for contractors and sub-contractors. In any event, the other warranties must not only be given, they must be in a similar form. For instance, if the architect has given a warranty that is expressed to be assignable in certain circum-stances, the other warranties must be similarly assignable. If the architect's warranty has a twelve year limitation period, the other warranties should have the same time limit.

6.27   As a further example, if a contractor has given a warranty in the following terms, it will avail the architect nothing: *The Contractor's liability to the Tenant hereunder shall be limited to liability in respect of defects appearing after practical completion which reasonable inspection by the architect at or before practical completion would not have revealed.* Assuming that the architect has been engaged to undertake normal site inspection duties, if reasonable inspection by the architect would have revealed the defects, the architect has been negligent in not discovering them. The effect of this clause is, therefore, that where the architect has negligently inspected, the contractor has no liability. The contractor may have given a warranty, but because of its terms the architect would not be able to obtain a contribution from the contractor.

6.28 A further possible solution to the problem of joint liability is to limit the consultant's liability (in circumstances where there is joint liability but not otherwise) to those cases where the others jointly liable have given effective warranties. This solution is less drastic than the 'condition precedent' clause referred to in paragraph 6.22, because if there is no joint liability, the architect's liability is unaffected by the existence or otherwise of other warranties. It does mean, though, that when there is joint liability the architect pays nothing if the others jointly liable have not given 'effective' warranties. This solution solves the first problem in paragraph 6.20 (of other warranties being given) and, depending upon the wording, may solve the second problem (of the insolvency of the others) also.

6.29 Another possible solution, and arguably the fairest, is what is called a 'net contribution clause'. The intention is that, whether other warranties have been given or not, and sometimes whether the others jointly liable can pay their share or not, the architect pays his 'net contribution', that is, the proportion that the architect would pay if he were able to obtain contribution under the Civil Liability (Contribution) Act 1978 from all relevant parties. Arguably, it is the share fairly attributable to his breach, referred to in the DTI Report quoted in paragraph 6.16. Some lawyers, however, consider that if in effect the clause requires the court to make an apportionment under the 1978 Act – in the absence of one of the parties who is jointly liable – the court has no jurisdiction to do so. Others consider that, so long as the intention is clear, the court should be able to give effect to the wishes of the parties.

6.30 Many different versions of net contribution clauses are seen in practice. There follow some examples, but none have so far been tested in court.

6.31 First, the two clauses that follow provide for net contribution if other warranties are not obtained, but the architect is still liable for 100% of the loss if another party jointly liable is unable to pay. They therefore deal with the first problem in paragraph 6.20 but not the second. *The Tenant hereby undertakes to obtain warranties in like terms hereto, from* [list those from whom warranties are to be obtained]. *Should the Tenant fail to obtain any or all of such warranties, the Consultant's liability to the Tenant shall be reduced by such amount for which the Consultant would otherwise have been entitled to recover by virtue of the Civil Liability (Contribution) Act 1978 from those persons from whom warranties have not been so obtained ...* Alternatively and more simply: *The Tenant shall obtain warranty agreements in similar terms from ... In the event that each of these agreements are not so entered into, the Consultant shall have no greater liability to the Tenant by virtue of this Agreement than it would have if such warranty agreements had been entered into.*

6.32   Secondly, in the following two examples, the architect is only liable for his net contribution even if the others jointly liable are unable to pay their contribution (thus these clauses seek to solve both the problems referred to in paragraph 6.20): *The amount of damages which the Tenant is entitled to recover from the Architect as a result of this Agreement shall be reduced in the following circumstances: the Architect shall be liable to the Tenant for no greater proportion of the full loss and damage suffered by the Tenant than that for which the Architect proves (on a balance of probabilities) that it would have been liable in contribution proceedings pursuant to section 1 of the Civil Liability (Contribution) Act 1978 between the Architect and any of* [the other consultants, contractor etc] *on the assumption (if it is not the case) that all parties to such contribution proceedings had entered into warranty agreements in substantially similar form to this Agreement and such warranty agreements were enforceable by the Tenant.*

6.33   The second example is: *The parties hereto specifically agree and acknowledge that the amount payable by the Consultant in respect of any liability hereunder to the Tenant shall not exceed the amount of his net contribution to the Tenant's damage after taking into account the actual or deemed contributions of the other relevant consultants and/or contractors employed on the Development and to the extent that the Tenant has failed to procure valid contracts from such relevant consultants and contractors with regard to their respective services, the onus shall be on the Tenant to establish that such failure has not prejudiced the ability of the Consultant to claim contribution from such relevant consultants or contractors.*

6.34   In the first three of the four clauses quoted in paragraphs 6.31 to 6.33 above it is anticipated that all the others from whom warranties should be obtained are listed. For the architect to be fully protected, the list should include any other party with whom he could be jointly liable (see paragraph 6.14).

7 Insurance considerations

7.01 In paragraph 5.47 it was said that those obtaining warranties will generally be relying upon the architect having professional indemnity insurance in the event of there being a sizeable claim. However, the architect will want the reassurance that there is insurance cover more than anyone.

7.02 Professional indemnity insurance is 'liability insurance', that is, the policy can be called upon by the insured architect in the event that he is liable to a third party. It also has one important characteristic: it is invariably underwritten on a 'claims made' basis. This should be contrasted with a 'claims occurring' policy, such as household insurance or a motor policy.

7.03 In a claims made policy, what is covered is claims made during the policy period. As most policies are renewable annually, this will usually be a year. Once the policy has lapsed, at the end of the year, the policy is inoperative. There will only be cover in respect of claims notified during the policy period.

7.04 Take the example of an architect who is engaged by his client in 1986 and carries out the design and inspection of a development over the next three years. In 1991 the client discovers hairline cracks in the external cladding and he writes to the architect blaming him and demanding that he do something about it. The architect should tell his insurers straightaway, and the relevant policy will be the one current when the notification is made, in 1991, not the one current when the mistake was made, say in 1987. If the architect had retired in 1990 and decided not to renew his policy, he would have no cover. If, on the other hand, he decided to raise his cover from £1 million to £5 million on renewal in 1991, the higher limit would apply.

7.05 The problem with claims made cover (both for the insured architect and anyone who might have a claim against the architect) is that it is not known from year to year what cover will be available. Say, in the example in paragraph 7.04, that on completion of the development in 1989 it was sold and the architect gave a warranty to the purchaser, who then wrote complaining about the cracks. The architect may have told his insurers about the warranty in 1989, but since the notification is given in 1991, he needs to be sure that his 1991 insurers will cover the claim.

7.06   Since executing warranties entails taking on obligations which he would not otherwise have, an architect must specifically check what information and details his insurers want about warranties, and what they will agree to cover. For example, they may want full details (and copies) of all warranties executed. Alternatively, they may not need special notice of warranties provided that they are in a certain form; and in relation to other warranties, they may have guidelines regarding what will be covered.

7.07   As has been said, professional indemnity insurance policies are generally renewable annually. Each year a new policy is taken out and a new contract is entered into between the architect and the insurer. The terms of the policy can therefore change from year to year. The architect needs to provide all necessary information upon each renewal (unless there is an agreement to the contrary). He will probably be dealing direct with an insurance broker, not with his insurer or underwriter. Although he may stay with one firm of brokers for his entire professional career, during that time there may be a number of changes of insurer. In any event, whether there is a change of insurer or not, upon each renewal the architect will need to check what cover he has for warranties.

8   Are there any alternatives?

8.01   Having come thus far, the reader might well ask whether there is not a better solution than warranties to the problem of allocating the risk of latent defects. In the short term, unfortunately, there are few alternatives, and none which solve the problem satisfactorily. In the long term, an alternative will surely have to be found.

Contractual alternatives

8.02   In the case of a purchaser, a developer might decide that instead of offering warranties he will assign the benefits of the consultants' appointments and the building contract to him. The purchaser is not given new, collateral, contracts but takes assignments of the developer's contracts. Therefore, when agreeing the terms of engagement, the developer will not ask the architect to give a purchaser warranty but it will be necessary to provide expressly that the appointment is assignable.

8.03   In the case of non-standard terms, the architect will want to consider his position carefully. For instance, if the developer has the right to assign the architect's appointment prior to completion of the works without the architect's consent, the effect is that he could require the architect to work with any purchaser to whom he sells the project. The architect might well want to have some control over the identity of his client, which he would only have if he was entitled to withhold his consent to the assignment. (See paragraph 5.67 for the difference between *with the Architect's consent* and *with the Architect's consent not to be unreasonably withheld*.) It is not unusual in non-standard terms of appointment for the architect to have only limited rights to terminate his engagement, so if his consent is not required he might have to work with the new client and complete his services, whether he likes it or not.

8.04   Different considerations apply when the development is complete. Once the architect has completed his services, the benefit of the appointment as far as the developer is concerned is the right to sue the architect if he has been negligent. The architect might well not want a third party, who was not his client during the design and construction period and who did not instruct and pay him, to be able to sue under the appointment. On the other hand, he might be prepared to give a warranty and there could be good reason for the architect preferring to do this. He might, for example, limit the damages recoverable to remedial works only (see paragraphs 5.34–5.38). If the purchaser took an assignment of the appointment, there would be no such limitation on the damages recoverable (but see paragraph 5.73).

8.05   The problem of joint liability (see section 6) should be addressed, if the appointment is assigned. Although the presumption is that where one consultant's appointment is assigned the other appointments and the building contract will also be assigned, if the 'network of contracts' is not preserved the architect could find that he is unable to recover contributions from those jointly liable with him (see paragraph 6.18). All the relevant contracts (which will vary depending upon the form of building contract and the contractual arrangements) should be assigned at the same time. Where JCT 80 is being used, for instance, a proviso could be added to the right to assign that any other consultants' appointments, the building contract and any sub-contractor warranties should be similarly and contemporaneously assigned.

8.06   In the case of tenants, it is unlikely that assignments of the consultants' appointments and building contract will be a practical alternative to warranties, unless possibly the development is let to one tenant. However, a tenant will only require warranties if he has the obligation, under his lease, to remedy latent defects. Although, therefore, commercial leases do commonly impose full repairing covenants on the tenant, if the landlord is prepared to retain the obligation to remedy latent defects rather than impose it on the tenant, there is no need for tenant warranties. Developers are generally, although not invariably, reluctant to do this.

Latent defects insurance

8.07   Traditionally, in the UK, it has been for each of the parties involved in a development to insure his own risks as best he can. Thus the professional team, the contractor, sub-contractors, owners and occupiers may all take out insurance to cover certain risks. A potentially more efficient form of insurance (for serious latent defects, in any event) is a policy covering the development itself. Such a policy is sometimes known as Building Users' Insurance against Latent Defects (BUILD) and it is becoming more widely available on the insurance market and more popular with developers.

8.08   It is a non-cancellable material damage policy for the benefit of the developer, subsequent owners and occupiers. Each policy is subject to its own terms but, generally speaking, it is only effective from practical completion. If, as a result of a design or construction problem, a defect occurs which is covered, recovery can be made under the policy without proof of fault. Historically the cover extended to no more than defects in the structure and the weatherproofing envelope. However, insurers have recently been prepared to offer additional cover for mechanical, electrical, heating and ventilating systems. The policy is usually for ten years (it is sometimes called a decennial policy), and covers claims arising from the cost of remedial works. The insurer generally wants the reassurance of a checking agency approving the design and monitoring the construction, so it is usually necessary to make the decision whether to take out such a policy at an early stage of the project.

8.09   One major concern for the architect will be whether he is covered by such a policy. This can be effected in two ways. First, he can be added as a joint named insured party or secondly (and more commonly) insurers can agree in the policy to waive their rights of subrogation.

8.10   Rights of subrogation are the rights that an insurer has (under an indemnity insurance policy), once he has paid out a claim, to step into the shoes of the insured and sue any party who is responsible for the loss in the insured's name. The insurer has the right to receive the benefit of all rights and remedies that the insured has against third parties. A common example is that of insurers seeking to recover the cost of underpinning necessitated by subsidence when they have paid out under a household policy. They will pay for the remedial works or reimburse the house owner, and they can then sue the contractor and architect who designed and constructed the foundations, in the householder's name. In the case of latent defects insurance, therefore, if the insurer does not waive his subrogation rights, the architect could find that he is in fact sued, not by his client, but by the latent defects cover insurer (although the remedy available to the insurer would of course be limited to that available to the insured party who originally suffered the loss).

8.11   Such a policy does not remove the need for warranties entirely,
         even if the professional team and contractor are covered. Not all
         losses, for example, will be recoverable under the policy. However,
         if the purchaser and tenants of a development know that they
         have the benefit of this insurance, the pressure for warranties
         should be eased somewhat.

Standard forms

8.12   Some of the problems created by warranties would diminish if
         there were readily accepted standard forms available. Section 4
         describes the forms which are currently available and what
         discussions are taking place with a view to standard forms being
         produced. In the meantime, warranties are negotiated on each
         different job between each party who is asked to give a warranty
         and each party who wants a warranty.

Legislation

8.13   In *Murphy* (see case notes, 9.02), the House of Lords indicated
         that it was for the legislature to determine the precise extent and
         limits of the liabilities which, in the public interest, should be
         imposed upon builders and local authorities. That case concerned
         a local authority, but the point is equally applicable in the case of
         consultants. If anything, following *Murphy,* the position for
         consultants is more uncertain than after the earlier case, *D & F
         Estates* (see case notes, 9.17).

8.14   One simple answer to the problem of putting warranties into place
         for each development would be for those who at present demand
         the protection of warranties to be given statutory remedies. The
         Defective Premises Act gives some rights in respect of dwellings,
         and further legislation dealing with all other types of buildings
         could provide the answer, although there would be keen debate as
         to what rights such legislation should give against whom. It is not
         easy to find Parliamentary time for this kind of legislation, even if
         there were any consensus as to what should be enacted. In the
         meantime the parties continue to legislate for themselves.

8.15   An additional factor is the European dimension. For some time
         the whole question of liability for latent defects in buildings has

been under discussion throughout the European Community following calls for the standardisation of contracts and controls in the construction industry. At present, the law in relation to latent defects varies dramatically between EC member states.

8.16　　It remains to be seen what the position will be in the UK in a few years' time. Will consultants, contractors, clients, financiers, purchasers, tenants and all the others still be negotiating warranties, or will they have become a thing of the past?

9 Case notes

9.01   In the preceding pages, mention has been made of a handful of landmark decisions which have shaped the law of tort over the last twenty years and there follows a brief summary of each of them. All are cases where the plaintiff was suing in tort and did not have a contract with the defendant. They appear in the order in which the judgments were delivered, with the most recent first.

Murphy v Brentwood District Council [1990] 2 AllER 908

9.02   Judgment was delivered in July 1990. The House of Lords took the exceptional step of overruling one of its earlier decisions, *Anns* (see paragraph 9.08). They also overruled the earlier Court of Appeal decision, *Dutton* (see paragraph 9.11).

9.03   Mr Murphy was the owner of a new semi-detached house in Brentwood, which had been built on a raft foundation. Before construction the plans and calculations had, in the usual way, been submitted to the local authority for building regulation approval. The council referred them to consulting engineers for checking and they approved the design. Some 11 years after he had purchased the house, Mr Murphy noticed cracks in the internal walls which, it was discovered, were caused by cracking of the raft due to differential settlement. As he could not afford the cost of repairs, he sold the house, and he got £35,000 less than the full market value. He therefore sued the council for this sum, alleging that their consulting engineers were negligent and that they were responsible for them. Although he was successful at first instance and in the Court of Appeal, he lost in the House of Lords.

9.04   The Law Lords held that the council owed Mr Murphy no duty of care in tort when it approved the foundation designs. A local authority was not liable to a building owner for the cost of remedying a dangerous defect in a building which resulted from the authority's negligence in approving the plans, but which became apparent before the defect caused physical injury. This was despite the fact that the Official Referee (a judge specialising in construction cases) who first heard the case, decided that Mr Murphy had been exposed to an imminent risk to health and safety. The damage suffered by Mr Murphy was purely economic loss and irrecoverable, it was decided.

D & F Estates Ltd & Ors v Church Commissioners for England & Ors [1989] 1 AC 177

9.05 This House of Lords decision was delivered in July 1988, two years before *Murphy*. It was a particularly unsatisfactory case, and many more questions were posed by the five judgments given by their Lordships than were answered.

9.06 The plaintiffs, D & F Estates Ltd, were the occupiers and lessees of flat 37, Chelwood House, which had been constructed in 1963–5 on land owned by the Church Commissioners. The flat was occupied by the directors of D & F Estates Ltd, Mr and Mrs Tilman. In 1980, while the flat was being decorated, it was discovered that the ceiling and wall plaster was loose, and some fell down causing minor damage to carpets. All loose plaster was then hacked off and replaced. The plaintiffs sued various defendants in tort, including the contractors, Wates. It was found that the plaster had been wrongly applied by the plasterers, who were Wates' domestic sub-contractors, and were not sued presumably because it was not considered worth while to do so. The damages claimed were some £100,000, being the cost of remedial works, etc. The Official Referee gave judgment for the plaintiffs, but they lost in the Court of Appeal and in the House of Lords.

9.07 It was held that the damages suffered had been purely economic loss, which was not recoverable in tort. The reasoning was that the defect in the plaster had been discovered before it had caused personal injury or damage to other property (apart from the minor damage to the carpets). Once the defect was discovered, the loss incurred in remedying it was purely economic, even if health and safety factors applied because it was a dangerous defect. Although this was a case involving the liability in tort of contractors, it is considered equally applicable to the tortious liability of architects.

Anns v Merton London Borough Council [1978] AC 728

9.08 This House of Lords' judgment was given in May 1977. The case was about the liability of the local authority for the negligence of their building inspector in exercising their powers under the building regulations to inspect foundations. Lord Wilberforce's twofold test for the existence of a duty in tort, enunciated in his judgment in this case, must have been cited in more cases in the last 13 years than any other judicial utterance. The test was: first, was there sufficient proximity between the parties that the wrongdoer might reasonably suppose that carelessness on his part may be likely to cause damage to the other; and if so, secondly, were there any factors which should negative or reduce liability? However, it was held in *Murphy* that this is not the appropriate test.

9.09   Mr Anns (and seven other plaintiffs) were long leaseholders of maisonettes in a block in Wimbledon. The defendant local authority had passed the drawings under the byelaws. However, structural movement in the flats resulted in cracks in the walls and sloping of floors. Mr Anns sued the London Borough of Merton on the basis that the building inspector allowed the builders to build the maisonettes with foundations only 2ft 6in deep instead of 3ft or deeper, as required by the deposited drawings. The argument was that the local authority had a duty to ensure that the block was built in accordance with the drawings.

9.10   It was held that the local authority had a duty to decide whether or not to make inspections and that when they did inspect, their obligation was to take reasonable care in so doing. It was also held that the cause of action in this type of case did not arise until the building was in a condition where it posed a present or imminent danger to the health or safety of the persons occupying it. The twofold test and timing of the accrual of the cause of action were widely held to apply to cases against architects and other professional consultants.

Dutton v Bognor Regis Urban District Council [1972] 1 QB 373

9.11   This case was decided by the Court of Appeal in December 1971, when Lord Denning was Master of the Rolls. Like two of the previous cases, it was about defective foundations and a local authority. As a result of this case many house owners (or their insurers) will have recovered damages from local authorities (or their insurers), but in July 1990 the House of Lords overruled it, in *Murphy*.

9.12   In 1960, Mrs Saidee Dutton bought a house in Bognor Regis for
        £4,800. Soon after she moved in, serious defects appeared inside,
        and the expert evidence was that the internal foundations were
        built on the site of an old rubbish tip. Mrs Dutton sued the
        builder and the local authority. She accepted £625 in settlement
        from the builder and continued the action against the council,
        alleging that they had been negligent in exercising their powers
        under the building byelaws. She won both at first instance and in
        the Court of Appeal, and obtained judgment for £2,115.

9.13   It was held that the local authority had a duty in tort to take
        reasonable care to see that the byelaws were complied with. Further,
        on the evidence, the approval of the foundations had been negligent.
        This resulted in the house being put on the market with a hidden
        defect likely to cause injury to a future purchaser and this was a
        breach of the common law duty. It was specifically held that the
        council's liability was not limited to damages for physical injury but
        extended to the damage to the house and might include economic
        loss. This can be directly contrasted with the more recent decisions.

Hedley Byrne & Co Ltd v Heller & Partners Ltd [1964] AC 465

9.14   This House of Lords decision is about a negligently given bank
        reference, and the judgment was given in May 1963. The case is
        distinct from those above, partly because it is the only one not
        concerned with construction. It established the 'reliance duty'
        category of liability in tort; a duty which can arise where there has
        been reliance on a statement given by someone possessing a special
        skill or knowledge. Some argue that there are two limbs of tort
        liability. One flows from *Donoghue v Stevenson* (the snail in the
        ginger beer bottle case, that was the foundation of the modern law
        of negligence) and the other from *Hedley Byrne*. The importance of
        the 'reliance duty' cases is that economic loss is recoverable as part
        of the damages, whereas in the other category of cases it is not.

9.15   Hedley Byrne were advertising agents, and they asked their bankers
        to enquire into the financial stability of a certain company with
        whom they were doing business. Their bankers made enquiries of
        the company's bankers, Heller & Partners Ltd. Heller gave a
        favourable reference, although they did qualify it by saying that it
        was *without responsibility*. In reliance upon the reference, Hedley
        Byrne placed orders, as a result of which they lost £15,454 3s 6d.

9.16   It was held that a negligent, though honest, mis-statement may give rise to an action for damages in tort for financial loss caused thereby, since the law implied a duty of care when a party seeking information from a party possessed of a special skill trusts him to exercise due care, and that party knew or ought to have known that reliance was being placed upon his skill and judgment. In this particular case, since there was an express disclaimer, no such duty was implied.

9.17   At the time of writing, one of the great uncertainties for professional people (such as architects) is the extent to which they owe *Hedley Byrne* type duties in tort to those who own and occupy buildings they have designed. In *Murphy,* Lord Keith suggested that they might do so. (He explained that the reason the engineers were liable in the well known case of *Pirelli v Oscar Faber & Partners* was because they owed a *Hedley Byrne* reliance duty to Pirelli.) However, the comment was not necessary to the decision and it remains to be seen what judges will do in future cases involving construction professionals rather than local authorities or builders.

9.18   As the preceding pages have demonstrated, the law is full of imponderables.

Index

Some legal terms are defined in the Glossary. 'Case law' collects together all references to individual cases. Statutes and subject topics are listed alphabetically.